Toward Endless Light

A Christian Writer's Spiritual Journey through Memoir

ANITA KRAAL-ZUIDEMA

WESTBOW
PRESS®
A DIVISION OF THOMAS NELSON
& ZONDERVAN

WestBow Press books may be ordered through booksellers or by contacting:

WestBow Press
A Division of Thomas Nelson & Zondervan
1663 Liberty Drive
Bloomington, IN 47403
www.westbowpress.com
1 (866) 928-1240

Because of the dynamic nature of the Internet, any web addresses or links contained in this book may have changed since publication and may no longer be valid. The views expressed in this work are solely those of the author and do not necessarily reflect the views of the publisher, and the publisher hereby disclaims any responsibility for them.

Any people depicted in stock imagery provided by Getty Images are models, and such images are being used for illustrative purposes only. Certain stock imagery © Getty Images.

Scripture quotations marked ESV taken from The Holy Bible, English Standard Version® (ESV®), Copyright © 2001 by Crossway, a publishing ministry of Good News Publishers. All rights reserved.

Scripture quotations marked MSG are taken from The Message. Copyright © 1993, 1994, 1995, 1996, 2000, 2001, 2002. Used by permission of NavPress Publishing Group.

Scripture quotations marked NRSV are from the New Revised Standard Version Bible, copyright © 1989 the Division of Christian Education of the National Council of the Churches of Christ in the United States of America. Used by permission. All rights reserved.

ISBN: 978-1-9736-6272-3 (sc)
ISBN: 978-1-9736-6273-0 (hc)
ISBN: 978-1-9736-6271-6 (e)

Library of Congress Control Number: 2019907140

Print information available on the last page.

WestBow Press rev. date: 6/24/2019

Author's Notes

Toward Endless Light … A Christian Writer's Spiritual Journey through Memoir, is a collection of essays seven or more years in the making. When I first started filing pieces under the heading *Living Green,* I had no greater purpose in mind other than to leave a love legacy for family. My daughters knew that if anything happened to me, they might enjoy reading some interesting pieces about themselves, my "big family" heritage, Grandpa K's immigration story, their mom going back to college—nearly forty years old—and their *super dad* who helped her accomplish it all. "Just open *Living Green,*" I said.

Now I was newly retired and pondering how to make my life count—beyond the volunteering, homemaking, and grandma stuff. Al was still very involved in all areas of life, so the decision was mine alone. How would I move forward with my life and not simply move on.

About this time I joined a writing memoir class through the Calvin Academic Lifelong Learning (CALL) program. I was already imagining *writing* as a new *profession*—paycheck exempt, of course. For someone my age, memoir should come with a more provocative and mature voice. I was both, provocative and mature—and now, excited to begin.

I reasoned, my grandkids might (someday) want to learn what Grandma Z thought would be helpful to know when they were hurting or questioning others or themselves and what they should do when they felt lost or unimportant. My word offerings would be an eye into their family history to the beat of a grandma's heart. And, what about their kids? My yet-to-be-born great-grandchildren?

As you can tell, God was calling me to a greater vision, and now I never wonder what to do with my time.

A little later, I was encouraged by a writing coach to sort out and publish articles I had already written on the topic of virtuous living, especially but not exclusively for women. My first book, *She Walks in Beauty and Endless Light*, fulfilled that mandate.

I grew into adulthood with the Vietnam War generation and Woodstock music and culture. Pete Seeger's "Where Have All the Flowers Gone?" comes quickly to mind as one of the popular hootenanny songs we sang, but I confess I was mostly looking past––not at the changing culture around me. Young. In denial. Not my problem.

Now I see that we, the flower children and me, were babes of innocence, feeling our way, sometimes blindly, through the land mines of a lost segment of society.

So what did we really want? What did we know, waaay back in the sixties and seventies—of another century?

I wonder if my grandchildren feel as insecure in this world as I did in mine. Their world, their parents' world, appears less stable—just a few decades later.

In *Toward Endless Light* I've tried to foster a greater appreciation and love for scripture and the biblical solutions it offers. I include quotations of wise scholars from the past who express deep thoughts and timeless truths. Each essay ends with thought-provoking questions meant to challenge us along the way. (Thanks, Helen, for your timely advice!)

I found myself unwittingly thinking of and writing for writers— not to advise, but to encourage. Most of us enjoy a pity party now and then. The most difficult part of completing this manuscript for publication was to acknowledge I was still searching for answers to the sort of questions that plague most of us, not just writers, at various times in our lives. Why was I spending so much time doing what maybe nobody or a rare few people would appreciate? Who really cares what I think, create, write?

My friends, my daughters, and my sisters will confirm that during this last year and a half, they have occasionally had to pull me out of my self-created dumpster. They help me clean up my attitude and set me back on track. Believe me, I fall prey to the same Qs that moms and dads ask themselves, doing the same mundane activities day after day. There are no easy As.

They rarely hear, "Good job, Mom. Great dinner!" "Thanks so much, Dad, for fixing my bike. Thanks for doing my laundry. For taking me to another practice. For sitting, on those cold, hard bleachers. And thanks for cheering me on!"

Most of life is accomplished without ready answers to our most difficult questions—the *Whys* and the *Why me* sort. When I'm honest with myself, I realize, it's often the devil—sitting on my shoulder, doing his very best to keep me from doing my very best. Thank God, he succeeds less and less—as I listen more closely to the only One who has answers to all my questions. They will come—in His time, in His way.

Let's be more purposeful "in word or deed [to] do everything in the name of the Lord Jesus, giving thanks to God the Father through Him" (Colossians 3:17 NRSV).

All the glory belongs to Him!

Dedication

From the day we met, fifty years ago, Al has been a faithful husband and the best helpmate any wife or writer could ask for. If you know him at all, you know that most of his life is dedicated to service. He'll do "leftovers" anytime and never makes me feel guilty for taking too much time at my desk. He's there for the little things and the big issues, particularly now, computer issues.

His heart is at home when he's making life better for his family, for his church, and for others. I'm forever grateful God brought him into my life.

Toward Endless Light

She unravels her life before His eyes, and then her own.
Retrieving, releasing simple and eloquent lore,
Buried deep in darkening tunnels of time.
She searches for threads that glitter and gleam
To tie up the prose of her life.

Bright threads to illumine the stonework
Of an invested, empowered existence.
Prized, rarer treasures blossom untamed
With pure and unabridged enchantment.
Still, she plumbs the depths of mystical shadows.

She probes the forgotten past with passion
And aspires for eager souls to join the advance.
Finally, she soars the heights of surrender,
Conquers fear and lack of courage
To celebrate the promise of a loftier yield.

She journeys faithfully up the illumined path,
With wings of prayer and grace.
Toward hope and peace and restorative resolution.
Saints and sinners saved, we converge,
Together, walking on toward endless light.
(2016)

Contents

Back Door to Success

> Success is to be measured not so much by the position one
> has reached in life as by the obstacles he has overcome.
> —Booker T. Washington

Reporters love to sleuth out amazing feats of endurance and determination, often in fields of human misery, where the potential for success or actual tragedy sits on the head of a pin.

Biographers with the propensity to access a life worthy of story inquire deep into a forgotten past, hoping to unleash the masterpiece or breakdown of that life. Most stories would be trivial if failures or heartaches were ignored. Failures tend to add a spicy element to what might otherwise be a bland dish. Where is *the story* if the trajectory of a life is simply up and up?

Lessons we learn during the process of overcoming difficult or painful experiences can strengthen us in the fight against shallowness and an untested existence. Without a proportionate wrestling match in the lowlands, few would realize the mental maturity to achieve authentic success.

As the story line of our life develops and matures, it will be up to us to retell what is worthy in a way that draws readers or listeners to the stories we were born to tell.

Kahlil Gibran, prestigious Lebanese American poet, artist, and writer, penned these prophetic words: "Out of suffering have emerged the strongest souls. The most massive characters are seared with scars."

Here is wisdom that drips with the blood, sweat, and tears of hard-pressed truth. Success comes at a high price but is almost always worth the effort.

The voluminous works of Mozart are riveting. Destructive and even mysterious forces, constantly at work in his brief life span of thirty-five years, birthed the passions and clamorings of his soul when he was destitute, unappreciated, and struggling to support his family.

As I studied his brief but amazing life, I found it obvious that Mozart's greatest compositions were born out of the anguish of stunning disasters and mental torment. Through it all, Mozart persisted. His music grew richer and deeper as it fought its way through to a hard but rocky surface.

Although ill and in constant pain, he persisted to finish one of the signature achievements of his life, *The Magic Flute*. It would be his final opera, and it was received with open arms by the townspeople of Vienna, his favorite place to live and work.

Only a few months later, while in the process of finishing a commissioned requiem, he was forced to pen these words:

> I have come to the end before having enjoyed my talent. Life was so lovely ... but one cannot change one's destiny. No one can know the measure of his days ... I end my days; here is my requiem which I must not leave unfinished.[1]

He did, however, leave this world before accomplishing that goal. Instead of a rollicking finale as he—or any of his prodigies or countless admirers—would have chosen for his exit, and at a much later date, his notoriously troubled existence and an unknown illness severed his career with an unfinished lament written for another's funeral.

Mozart never knew the impact his life and accomplishments would have on world history or the joy he would bring to thousands of eager and diligent students who have since studied and loved his vast catalogue of music.

The realities of life confirm for us that when the wind is fierce,

---

[1] Michel Parouty, *Mozart: From Child Prodigy to Tragic Hero* (Harry N. Abrams, Inc., Publishers, 1993), 127.

when it pelts your face like shards of glacier ice, when you have to fight with every ounce of physical and mental strength to secure the goal or jump the next hurdle, you need only to breathe a prayer of thanks and ask for strength for the moment and for the day. Let's pray for joy on the journey, knowing that success and heaven await the faithful follower.

Let's be thankful and grateful for the efforts of those in our support system—parents, teachers, coaches, friends, teammates, and anyone else who has willingly walked alongside us. Their prayers rose when ours were lost in self-pity.

Something to Ponder

> What is your definition of success? Do you have something in your life that has cost you much but is worth the price?
> What story lies dormant in your memory bank that would make a positive difference for someone facing one of life's difficult challenges?

Finishing Well

Publishing was a huge learning curve last summer, but I'm so glad I persisted to *just do it!* Truthfully, I wanted to *just fuhgeddaboudit!*

Seven plus years' worth of essays are listed under the header *Living Green*. About a third of them were used for *She Walks in Beauty and Endless Light*. Now it's time to dig up and clean up the rest of these *babes in waiting.*

I'm thinking about the next writing project: the one you hold in your hands.

The concept of living green is a gentle reminder to be in constant pursuit of God's will and plan through all seasons of life, with all their tangled interfaces. Whether celebrating the vibrancy of youth with all its budding possibilities or feeling mature, secure, and at the top of our game, the pungency of autumn breezes beckons us, and we realize that the final chapter here on earth is not simply for the old and weathered to consider.

Most of us know the names and faces of family or close friends who left us far too soon. We also know that any one of us could be perched on a rocky ledge for an inclement season or two. Illness, insecurity, and displacement—emotional or otherwise—cause us to question everything and everyone around us. Sometimes, we question God.

Like winter's frigid blast, adverse circumstances often serve to chase us back to the Rock and Fortress we too quickly forget is there for us—always and forever (Psalm 18:2).

The flesh may be weak, but the Spirit who rides on and conquers the storms, without and within, is able to redirect our steps and demolish our strongholds (2 Corinthians 10:4–5). But we must be willing to fight hard for the gold and finish the race set before us. After all is said and done, we have the gift of the Spirit to finish well.

Living Bold and Audacious

I've hit another milestone, Lord,
with yet another choice to make:
To climb a few more mountains
or retire and put this busy mind to rest.
Then comes His clear but quiet voice. *I've called you*
To leave a legacy of words and thoughts to ponder.

Moving forward, I start the daunting climb
renewed. Emboldened. Audacious.
Ready to begin and seize the day,
to leave a gift of gentle thoughts and challenges.
I'll need to learn a few new things, Lord.
Writing is fun, but publishing? Not so much.
My wrinkled brain groans and rebels. So for now,
I take a few slower steps.

Then by faith, I'm moving on and forward.
Emboldened. Audacious.
Walking always toward the Light, and soon,
it's time to rest.
So come and sit with me, dear friend.
We'll linger and enjoy each milestone.
The view from the top will be amazing,
and faith's reward awaits the victor.

Something to Ponder

➢   When we are in fellowship with God, we can leave winter's bleakness behind to find a lasting springtime of joyfulness. Is that true for you?

➢   If you have experienced God's love and faithfulness during a difficult season of your life, give God the glory. Then share God's love with someone who needs to know you care.

➢   If you are hurting, reach out to a friend or spiritual mentor who can help you find fellowship with the One who created you and knows you inside and out. He wants you to give it all over to Him. Why? "Because He cares for you" (1 Peter 5:7 NRSV).

Devoted or Distracted

> I am saying this for your own benefit, not to lay any
> restraint upon you, but to promote good order and
> to secure your undivided devotion to the Lord.
> —1 Corinthians 7:35 (ESV)

When sleep eludes and fearsome thoughts threaten to overtake my sanity, I call a halt to the whirligig, pull on a cover-up, and find my way to an always welcoming prayer chair. All my unfocused questions and unresolved worries can quickly be routed if I consciously direct my steps to the Word and, often, a favorite devotional.

Tonight, I settle into the Word alongside Oswald Chambers, late-eighteenth-century gifted artist and trained musician. Oswald was converted under Charles Haddon Spurgeon during his teen years. Oswald literally gave his young Scottish life to become an ambassador for Christ as an international traveling Bible teacher in the early 1900s.

Chambers, who straddled the turn of the twentieth century, shares the distinction of having lived the same brief but productive life span as Alexander the Great and his own divine mentor, Jesus Christ. It is humbling to look at the major accomplishments these men left in a fleeting thirty-three years. Alexander left an unprecedented legacy of human achievements and was best known for greatly expanding and advancing Greek culture. The proverb "I am not afraid of an army of lions led by a sheep; I am afraid of an army of sheep led by a lion" is often attributed to Alexander the Great. The value and immensity of Oswald's life's work was realized and carried forward by his gifted wife. Biddy was a court stenographer who had taken verbatim shorthand of every speech her Oswald ever gave. Refusing to be distracted, she worked tirelessly for the next fifty years, devoted to the work of transcribing her husband's speeches. She is credited with breaking down some of them into palatable daily reflections, which are compiled in the classic devotional *My Utmost for His Highest* (1935).

This Christian classic, wonderfully updated in 1992, is as fresh today as in 1935. Under Biddy's devoted care, more than thirty book titles followed, to "give his words to the world."

Chambers was known for startling his audiences with his "vigorous thinking and vivid expression." Even now, reading his devotionals is not for the fainthearted. I often find myself caught up, forgetful of time, winnowing away at the profound wisdom of the day's topic, or even a single paragraph.

Today's entry is June 18. It is 11:50 PM. When I close the book, it will be June 19, 12:45 AM. As I fitfully read that day's devotional, I am reminded that total abandonment of my will to His is mandatory if I am to complete the work God has called me to do.

Becoming a published writer has become a formidable call on my life, even while it seemed, at first, to be just one more grandiose pipe dream—more unrealistic than achieving a master's degree twenty-five years ago!

Is it possible that God would still expect the unexpected from me, now seventy years of age? Silly question. As I thought of the heroes of faith, Moses, Aaron, Elijah, Paul, and John (who wrote the Book of Revelation when he was ninety), I (oh me of little faith) knew the answer.

I love my quiet home life, but now, I'm swallowed up in the crucible of editing, revising, rewriting ... all to get ready for publishing—a second time. With daily distractions of family, church responsibilities, mental and emotional quandaries, and an aching back begging to exchange an office chair for a comfy lounge chair ... it is never easy.

So let's get real. Life is not meant to be easy or to celebrate self. It's meant to be used up and lived to the full measure of our days—to the glory of God.

Something to Ponder

> Feel free to pursue the maxim: *I am not afraid of an army of lions led by a sheep; I am afraid of an army of sheep led by a lion.* How does that relate to our Savior? If you need help, look up these wonderful verses: Isaiah 53:6–7; Micah 5:4–5; Matthew 15:24, 18:12–14; Revelation 5:5–6.

> Can you imagine staying focused for fifty years (like Biddy) to finish something your spouse or family member left unaccomplished?

> What does Biddy's gift teach us about dedication, determination, and never letting go of a worthy goal, no matter how long it takes?

The Writer's Garden ... Bringing Word Jewels to the Sunlight

To lose track of our stories is to be profoundly impoverished,
Not only humanly, but also spiritually.
—Frederick Buechner

A cold and drizzly rain reminds me. It is time to dig up and discard or repot those special geraniums that survived the move from Green Lake to Byron Center.

Summer in our new condo has ended. The move has been long and arduous, as many of us grayheads have experienced, but the blessings of sharing life with good neighbors, less upkeep, and plenty of patio space, not to mention the common green space with its unusual variety of trees, make it all worthwhile.

I've had great fun entertaining neighbors, old friends, and grandchildren these past few months. All around the patio we have plenty of room to add in our favorite plants for color. Massive tuberous begonias are an exciting addition to the variety of shade-loving astilbe and hostas thriving alongside our repotted geraniums—all transplanted from our gardens on the lake.

A towering hibiscus stands tall and healthy in the sun, its root system having endured Al's terrible hacksaw beating before we moved; he was determined to take only half, not the whole, of this root-bound giant.

My mother always repotted her favorite geraniums in late fall, bringing the best of them indoors for color in the dark days of winter. They would serve as starters for next year's garden.

Brilliant peach and crimson geraniums, indulged and carefully tended, are no longer showstoppers, and cold winds urge us to get this task accomplished. Al will dig, and I will repot what is worthy of a wintertime haven. It's our ritual for holding on to bits of summer till the smell of springtime earth beckons us outdoors and into the backyard again.

As leaves rustle down and half-naked tree limbs shiver, I

recognize the clarion call to join with nature and prepare for the changing of the guard. The dumpster around the corner is redolent of summer's decaying detritus. It's nearly filled with neighbors' garden refuse.

***

I brew another heady cup of java and settle into my writing corner. I'm eager and ready to continue the sweet but sweaty process of story-time gardening—reaching deep into the past to share the goodness of God in our lives and to honor Him with a writer's love offering.

Uncovering stories to resonate with the next generation sometimes demands digging deep into hard-packed and inhospitable ground. Although our lives may be bursting with hidden beauty, the viable core of a life story can be hunkered down and hidden in nasty weeds—virulent weeds, such as bitterness or misunderstandings or loss. Emotional wounds are part of the past for most of us.

Now, with God's help, we'll redeem what is healthy and let go of anything not worth salvaging. Into the dumpster it goes. No regrets. We'll forgive. We'll ask for forgiveness. Then we'll move on and move ahead—in our goals and in our aspirations for the future.

The writer of Colossians 3:13–14, in The Message, tells us to be "quick to forgive … as quickly and completely as the Master forgave you. And regardless of what else you put on, wear love." Love, he says, is "your basic, all-purpose garment. Never be without it."

If we have accepted the gift of salvation—Christ's gift of love—we are compelled to tell the stories of grace at work in our lives. Like the geraniums Mom painstakingly repotted, watered, and tended, these stories can be lovingly repotted to bloom again, outside our door.

Where is the story of God's grace in your life buried? Dig it out.

Then, with all the love in your heart, celebrate it, and tell your story to anyone who will listen.

Write this down [tell your stories] for the next generation,
so people not yet born will praise God.
—Psalm 102:18 (MSG)

Something to Ponder

➤ The tools you will need for story-time gardening could be one or all of these:

  o A heavy-duty spade—for digging deep into hard-packed soil and snarled root systems.

  o Heavy-duty gloves—to untangle healthy story starters from the weeds and to repot them into a new setting.

  o A huge trash bag—you will certainly dump more than you keep.

  o A suitable coverall—so you aren't afraid to get down and dirty and are ready to deal with the weeds, even if they're compacted and wedged in tight.

  o A discerning eye—for a good story, and a heart willing and ready to share it.

  o A creative imagination—to take a story to the finish line.

  o An attractive container—plant your stories with love, and they will bloom for you and others in the dead of winter or the driest desert.

Moving On or Moving Forward

But recall the former days when, after you were enlightened,
you endured a hard struggle with sufferings.
—Hebrews 10:32 (ESV)

Writing is, for the serious writer, a complicated, often lonely pursuit. Writing memoir, particularly, can be messy and murky for those who resolve to give back a legacy of well-chosen words and stories.

Mark Twain, after six years of haunting failure to accomplish his most engaging work, *Huckleberry Finn*, found remarkable success when he finally came to terms with the ominous shadows of his life. Bringing deep truths of a troubled past to light, in the character of Huck, released in him the energy and aspiration he needed to finish the project.

We all have demons that hold us hostage and keep us from moving forward. Yes, we all know how to *move on*; that happens quite naturally. But to *move forward*, there has to be significant, energetic, and productive action. That often comes at a price.

So, thinking about my *writer's garden*, I will dig, water, and weed. I will add a hint of fertilizer and prune away the useless or misguided vines of life story. We will replant worthy memories into story form and smile or laugh together when they bloom on the page. When hard truths find their way to the surface, we will be encouraged to grow, emotionally and spiritually.

Many of the stories in this memoir of *spiritual journeying* have uncovered events and defining moments from a treasure trove that has lain deep inside, untended, for many years. Looking back with purpose allows me to present past events from a decidedly matured perspective. That is, as our book's title suggests, we will choose to move forward—*Toward Endless Light*.

Know that every word is spilled out with love. Affirmative memories have imaged themselves in bold colors in my mind's eye and have been nurtured and indulged in the way of a gardener with precious seeds and plants. Precious and tender story saplings were sometimes pruned so the trunk of the story could grow strong and remaining branches could offer up a better yield.

We will recount the bountiful blessings God gave but also share lessons learned in wastelands of rebellion, remorse, or rejection. Their value far exceeds the distress of first recollection.

Something to Ponder

- ➢ I encourage you to recount what God has done in your own life. Start a journal, tape your stories for the next generation, write letters, or share a story in a Bible study or discussion group.
- ➢ Bring your stories to the family round table, or put them in bedtime story form for your little ones. Be sure to add a little spice and lots of zest.
- ➢ Remind yourself of God's handiwork shining through your life stories, and let others see it.
- ➢ What stories from the past could you tell now, that you couldn't have told earlier?
- ➢ What lessons have you learned to make the stories valuable and worth sharing?

Mom's Dream

The mind replays what the heart can't delete.
—Yasmin Mogahed

There were three kids when we moved in and another on the way. A big family, by today's standards. By her own words, Mom "never intended more than two." She knew the responsibility of a large family. She had helped raise eleven younger sibs on a very active farm. She might also have predicted that Dad—city-born and bred, the only son of doting parents, with one older, doting sister—wasn't best suited to father a large family.

Looking back, I know the Lord blessed Mom's stubborn determination to buy that little twenty-five-acre farm. Could there have been a better way or better place for Mom and Dad to raise their family and be able to support a Christian school education for eight growing youngsters (though she couldn't yet know the count)?

I assume she was reading the *Holland Evening Sentinel* "Homes and Farms for Sale" section when she found exactly what she was looking for. Better yet, in foreclosure. After that, Mom was absolutely driven. One determined Henny Penny.

Mom had foresight, which far outweighs hindsight, although the final number of her children would not have borne this out. I can't even imagine what we all would have missed had we not had each other to enjoy Mom's little piece of heaven. That minifarm was the lifeblood of our family, and our city-raised dad soon learned to love it.

Dad must have been scared witless by the prospect. He only knew what the word *farming* meant to his tall, spindly, but tough brothers-in-law. Personally, he was A-OK with working his factory job.

Fortunately for Mom and all of us, Dad was willing to come home from his day job to do what needed to be done at home. There was a cow to milk and maybe a pig to feed, twelve acres to plow, cultivate, and plant with corn, and a substantial garden for strawberries. There were cucumbers to pick (we called it "picking pickles") and much more. Off season, there would be wood to cut and haul out of the backwoods to keep the home fires burning.

Many stories could be told about the meandering creek that graced our property and the woods that wound itself around the creek basin. The boys spent hundreds of hours hunting and fishing, catching turtles, swimming, and all things *boys*. I know the younger girls often followed along, but this is not a familiar part of my story.

Helping Mom inside with cooking, cleaning, taking care of babies—this naturally resonated with my being the oldest but also with my temperament. During the crop and garden seasons, we all pitched in to get the jobs done.

A long, skinny chicken coop provided Mom with a familiar way to bring in cash. She raised chicks (we called them *peeps*) to the nine-week stage, just as she had done earlier at the farmhouse we rented from Grandpa B. The cycle started over every nine weeks. The chicks were soft, cuddly, and so cute—special to all of us, at least for a few weeks.

We always had chickens for eggs and eating. Once the hens stopped laying, Sunday dinner was fair game. One of my least favorite memories is of the chopping block behind the barn, where we'd watch Mom or Dad ax off the chickens' heads.

Watching the bloody, headless carcass flop around behind the barn was the inevitable aftermath of this gory scene. A clear case of animal cruelty, in today's jargon. Even so, it was impossible to watch the first act and not be glued to the second. First, the chopping, then the flopping. I was wide-eyed every time.

Next came the boiling water bath so Mom could pull the feathers off. And finally the gutting process. The putrid smell—indescribable. Unforgettable.

I promised myself and Mom, "When I get married, I will *never, ever* be part of this horrific activity again!"

Mom would laugh and say, "You'll get used to it. How else are you going to feed your family?"

I told her I'd buy my chicken all cut up and packaged. An addendum to that would be, "I will never boil chicken for dinner. It will be the fry pan, oven, or grill." I kept that promise, but the smell of boiled chicken lingers on.

Mom's little piece of heaven had a real barn. It was a child's dream playhouse. Many happy hours were spent with kids jumping from the rafters, just being kids. Our city cousins remember this as a highlight of any weekend they could visit. That, along with Mom's homemade bread, hand-churned butter, and (occasionally) hand-churned ice cream made the three-mile bicycle trip worth the effort. Add strawberries, and you will know the delight of a real strawberry ice cream sundae.

Below the hay mound was a stall for our one and only Jersey cow. Dad had to learn how to milk Bessie, probably in short order. I wonder if Mom taught him. Or might it have been a brawny brother-in-law? I seem to remember Dad cutting and nailing together his one legged milking stool. When Bessie stopped producing milk for the family's demands, which included butter, homemade ice cream, and mounds of whipping cream, she met the butcher's block in Grandpa's barn. Once chopped up and canned, she gave Mom some quick and easy suppers to her advantage. Soon after, Bessie # 2 would be *installed*. (Did you catch the pun?)

Occasionally Dad would purchase a piglet from one of the uncles. Once fattened up, it added some smokin' good ham, bacon, and pork chops to the menu.

Our front yard was not part of Mom's dream, I'm quite sure. It was the early 1950s, and most farmyards were not mowed, with the possible exception of an occasional "hay-raking."

Initially, the front yard was a field of scraggly orange daylilies growing wild. Mom eventually persuaded Dad to mow it all down for a semblance of green lawn. I remember walking on it, but only once. Too sharp, and very prickly for bare feet—and who didn't have bare feet in summertime?

Then there was a goat that served as lawn mower, but that might have been later.

When I think of how determined Mom was and how hard she worked to actuate and build on her dream, and at what price, it humbles me. Her dream really was about making a good life for her family, but, by God's amazing provision, it was big enough to include all eight of us.

Something to Ponder

➢ What dreams have you worked to turn into reality in the past? And now?

➢ What would you say is your greatest accomplishment to date?

➢ So … what's on your bucket list for the future?

➢ Are your dreams big enough?

Words to Change the World

Let the words of my mouth and the meditation of my heart
Be acceptable in Your sight,
O Lord, my strength and my Redeemer.
—Psalm 19:14 (NKJV)

I love words. I love the twists and turns and endless discretion they provide—when I speak and when I choose a card that expresses my thoughts perfectly, and when I sit down to write and pound out the thoughts of my heart in a journal or on my keyboard.

Words are powerful. Poorly chosen words can discourage, harden, or turn away a needy heart. Words well chosen can open a heart's door, previously shut tight.

I love the reward of rephrasing a sentence or paragraph till it gleams with clarity and precision. I love my thesaurus when I'm looking for exactly the right word to use.

Attending grad school in my early forties, I recognized once again why I preferred essay exams. Multiple choice tests seemed trite and unfulfilling—except for the person who has to do the grading. Essays demand a better understanding of the whole than A, B, C, or D. Serious students like me know the difference.

I suspect I inherited my passion for words from my mother, who was never frugal with words. I learned early on that words put together to form sentences and then paragraphs on colorful pages, in a book you could hold, had the power to transport you to another world. I would listen intently to every word and voice inflection of whoever answered my continual request to "tell me a story."

I begged to hear stories over and over, determined to retain the words of each page in my memory bank. It wouldn't be long before I would be able to "read it myself." Like all children, I wanted an audience to listen to my dramatic retelling of the story.

Doting aunts and Mom would say I talked in complete

sentences at a very young age to anyone, anywhere, and about anything. I also remember stories shared by aunts who were only a few years older. Stories from their schoolbooks. Young readers need young listeners, and I know they found an avid listener in me.

There was little time for books in Mom's life. Her greatest disappointment might have been that she was only allowed to finish eighth grade before being pulled out to work in the sewing factory. She handed over her check directly to Grandpa till the day before she married.

Mom was determined to instill a love of books and learning in her children. Sunday afternoon was her favorite time to read—to herself and her little ones. She would sit by the kitchen table, one arm propped under her chin, deeply absorbed in her one and only incoming magazine, *The Banner*—our church weekly. It was her window to a much larger world than where she lived and served her family, church, and school.

She read silently while the younger ones circled about the kitchen, involved with their own childish activities—none of which come to mind, other than an occasional pots and pans band. This probably would not have rattled Mom.

When she turned to the children's page, she would gather us around to hear the missionary story that bonded us to our Indian cousins in Rehoboth, New Mexico. She loved the missionaries and their stories and never gave up the desire to be one. She followed them to hear them speak at various churches and at the Christian Reformed Conference grounds.

Her heart would journey with them to faraway places. Her letters, included with her checks, helped them accomplish what she and other faithful followers commissioned them to do.

Late in the evening, when little ones were bedded down and it was finally quiet enough for me to do my homework or study for a test, Mom would sometimes find a few minutes to read. Both of us sat quietly at the kitchen table, lost in our own world of words.

Her book choices from the church library might have been

my first teen novels. Historical novels and nonfiction became my favorite books to read, then and now.

***

Some of our seven grandchildren have since used the same or similar phrase as I or their mothers did. They say, "Let me read it myself," long before they are able to decode the words.

We listen proudly as six-year-old Scarlett "reads" R o b e r t Munsch's *The Sand Castle Contest* to us. She turns the pages of this word-intense and lengthy learning tool, absorbed in the pictures, speaking with great expression and accuracy. Tomorrow she will take *Sand Castle* back to school. She will read the whole book to her kindergarten friends for show and tell. Her teacher and classmates will be impressed. Her delivery will be punctuated with great hand and body flourishes and voice articulations—just like her mother teaches her.

Preschool Scarlett loved to "highlight the words" with all her favorite colored markers. We smiled as she pored over a *Words of Hope* devotional booklet she chose to highlight "special words" to her heart's content.

This same grandchild seems to be holding on to her status symbol of being the youngest of the grandkids and of her own family, but now and then we stand amazed at the adultness coming out of our latest bright star. She definitely intends to take her place and change her world. Early on in her elementary years, she announced that girls should be allowed to preach in our church. She gave us fair warning: *"You better work on it, 'cuz I'm going to be preaching on that stage!"*

I'm too politically correct to weigh in publicly on this matter, but I'm going to encourage her to keep working on how to use her sharp wit and wisdom to change her world, if only by one word at a time.

Something to Ponder

> ➤ JK Rawling says, "Words are ... our most valuable source of magic." Why do, or don't, you think this is true?
> ➤ Do you remember when words on a page took on new or special meaning for you?

Life Savers

One of the greatest titles in the world is parent,
and one of the biggest blessings in the world
is to have parents to call Mom and Dad.
—Jim DeMint, Conservative Partnership Institute

Mom was an expert bread maker, with lots of experience from her growing-up years. We can't forget the heady smells of rising dough and the fun of rolling hamburger buns or cutting the thick, rough-hewn slices of fresh baked bread to slather with homemade butter and strawberry jam.

Still, with all those mouths to feed, Mom needed a little help. We loved it when the Colonial bread truck circled round our drive. Mom usually gave in to something special for an afternoon snack, and the driver always had a *good special* to tempt her.

More often, though, she picked up what was needed at the day-old bread store. Besides bread for school lunches, she would bring home staples such as Rusk hamburger buns and just plain Rusk—still served in many homes. We liked to soak it in hot milk, then add sugar and sometimes cinnamon.

Rusk was beyond optional for crumbling into Grandma K's recipe for making Dutch hamburgers: just mix ground beef, milk, egg, crushed Rusk, salt, and pepper, and don't forget nutmeg. Best burgers ever. We didn't have a grill, but hamburgers on Rusk buns on a Saturday night—who could ask for more?

It was certainly all Dad ever asked for. As long as hamburger, in any form, was on the table, Dad was a happy man.

***

Mom was working part-time by the time I was old enough to start babysitting, around eleven years of age. It was usually a night shift, so Dad would be home, but I pretty well took the lead, since

I don't remember Dad ever changing diapers, fixing any meals or bottles, or putting little ones to bed. During and after pickle season, Mom worked nights at Heinz Pickle Factory and much later at—you guessed it!—the Life Saver factory, built just prior to our wedding in 1968.

Seasonal or part time, it was just another sweet way to meet the high cost of Christian school tuition. By the time I graduated high school, Mom and Dad were only to the halfway mark of tuition driven years.

The Thrift Shop was another frequent stopover, and definitely a life saver—for Mom and (little did we appreciate it) for us. Essentially, all our clothes came from there. Mom chose quality brands to last for more than one wearing and possibly for more than one daughter. She was willing to pay a bit more because she refused to pay for junk.

Mom easily shared her life, her joys, and her woes with other women, so whatever job she held, her coworkers served as a support system and a lifeline.

It wasn't easy for her to leave the chaos at home, but unwinding with other women was probably more valuable than we realized. It was a way for her to gain a broader perspective—and served as another tether through the storms of her life.

When Mom finally headed home from wherever, it was always in a rush and always late. I remember standing at the kitchen window—with dinner ready, warming on the stove—often, for hours. At times, Dad and I would be standing side by side, watching for headlights and a turn signal. She rarely used them.

Occasionally, on a Friday or Saturday night, Mom would come home from grocery shopping, with fried smelt, ready to eat and such a treat! Of, course, we wouldn't know until she got home, since cell phones weren't a blip on anyone's screen.

Whatever was waiting in the oven would serve as side dishes to the smelt and fries. No worry about leftovers in this family.

After I left home, Mom worked at a laundromat, allowing

her to simultaneously do the family laundry while keeping the place clean and running smoothly. Next door was the beauty salon where she got her hair done every week. With Family Fare grocery store conveniently located in the same block, Mom looked for opportunities to chat and fill her mind with interesting conversations and ideas. If we had to find her, we knew she would be somewhere in this square block of *one-stop shopping*.

Years later she would spend happy hours volunteering at Bibles for Mexico, next door to Family Fare. Come to think of it, the mechanic who serviced Mom's cars for many of her driving years was directly across the street. He would have lots of interesting Mrs. Kraal stories if he were alive today!

***

When our uncle Jack's 15 Cent Hamburgers came to town, we had something else to wish for on weekends. I can taste that burger, still—catsup, mustard, and pickle, all on a wonderful squishy bun. Mom (never fond of hamburgers) must have struggled with this, but it was a time saver, so why complain?

Somehow, we never compared the fifteen-cent hamburg to the hand-mixed hamburgers we had at home. If we could eat out, quality didn't matter all that much.

I remember coming home from college on weekends to open a box of Appian Way or Chef Boyardee Pizza Mix—crust (just add water) and a can of pizza sauce included. Mozzarella cheese and crumbled, uncooked hamburger often topped this favorite. Greasy, but so good!

***

Mom had cared for her eleven younger sibs right up until she married Dad, and a year later she started her own child-rearing days. Her six sisters spent welcome hours at our house. They and her five brothers were an important lifeline for Mom, and her Brink ties held tight to the end.

Aunt Carolyn remembers helping out whenever her nursing schedule allowed. In return, Mom and Dad would give her some needed spending money. The three youngest sisters were only a few years older than me, and they were always welcome.

***

Sewing was a never-ending task, particularly once the canning season was over. A garment finished meant another pattern had to be laid out, and a mountain of fabric lay waiting to be cut.

Gingham checked fabric was popular for little girls' dresses, and Mom loved to use the smocking technique on gingham for the bodice. But how much time would this mom have had for *any* kind of craft stitching? If you add in the midnight hours—whatever your heart (or simple necessity) dictates.

"Still some coffee on the back burner, Mom?"

Many of Mom's sewing accomplishments took shape during these all-nighters. Did she have a coffee addiction to get her through? For many years, by her own admission, the answer was yes.

Do we really have to ask why? Knowing its response time in my own life, especially at my writing desk, I readily admit, coffee is a major life saver! In summer's heat, I'll let the second cup cool down—add ice cubes, a little cream, and I'm off and running.

Dresses, skirts, Dutch costumes, curtains or valences, even boys' Sunday jackets. Weddings meant burning the midnight oil, slumped over her sewing machine. Through her early married years, eleven younger sibs, one by one, eventually found their lifelong mates, so it must have seemed there was always a wedding in the works.

Her own eight goslings would soon start down the red carpet, and the trend continued. Several of my younger sisters became involved with the Klompen Dancers. Full regulation Dutch costumes were required. Mom was up for it, as always. Needless to say, there was always more sewing to be done.

I can't remember Mom unhappy to start another sewing project. She loved her sewing and her sewing machine, maybe as much as gardening. When Judy and I had our double wedding, Mom sewed the little blue jacket and pants for one of two ring bearers and all four sisters' dresses, including Debbie's flower girl dress.

Judy and I have different perspectives on our duple wedding day, but all in all, that great big double wedding saved time, money, and more stress than any of us could have handled. A life saver, for sure, for us and for our parents.

In all my years, I have never met anyone who shared our experience of a "twice nice" wedding. It was fun. It was crazy. There were many tears—of anxiety and (later) of joy. Then sighs of relief and absolute exhaustion.

This year we celebrate fifty years of marriage, and we can thank God that what was joined together stuck together!

***

While brother Bob was in Vietnam, Mom faithfully wrote letters to him. When I was on a summer mission team (SWIM), she wrote faithfully. I'm sure many of these letters were written in the wee small hours of the morning.

Following Mom's lead and remembering how she put those extra midnight hours to work for her, I still value the quietness of the midnight hour as my special time to "pull ahead" on whatever threatens to take me down. Even if it means I have to drag myself out of a warm bed.

I never would have made it through twelve years of advanced studies without tapping those precious midnight hours. For me, it's the gift that keeps on giving.

***

Mom was probably the least spoiled woman I've ever known. I have no idea how she survived and in some ways thrived as she moved through her teen years—the ever ready caregiver for a very large family—right on into the newlywed years, starting her own family, immediately after her first anniversary. Mothering was the only life she ever knew.

Too soon, at age seventy (two years younger than I am today) she became a widow with no one to cook for or care for but herself. Simultaneously, she had to fight colon cancer and the stress of selling her little farm—with all her kids clamoring for her to get rid of all the stuff of her meager worldly existence.

Once established in her condo, she had a hard time adjusting to a lack of worthwhile activities to pursue, so she quickly volunteered for other residents' needs—washing and ironing, driving to doctor appointments, and bringing homemade soup to someone under the weather.

Several years later, she would experience the fears and frustrations of facing a giant she would never overcome in this life. How frightening Alzheimer's must have been to her.

None of us can really relate—except that we ourselves are growing older. We have our own idiosyncrasies, our own issues—and our own kids to (dare I use the word) contend with.

One would think this a sad ending for one so selfless, but God has His way of making things right. Second Timothy 4:8 (NRSV) tells us there is a "crown of righteousness" waiting for "all who have longed for His appearing." I'm quite sure we will all be surprised at the crown covering Mom's beautiful white hair.

Something to Ponder

> Stop and think about it: a mom is God's first gift of a life saver to us. No mom? No you. No me.
> Can you think of a few life savers your mom put to use to make her own and the family's life better or easier?
> What do you recognize in your life to be life savers or time savers? (Try to stay away from including technology tools of any sort.)

Coming to America

There are far better things ahead than any we leave behind.
—C. S. Lewis

The Dutch are proud of their history and their many contributions to their new homeland, most having come by ship a century or more ago. Tulips blooming in May and Klompen (wooden shoe) Dancers, parades and festive songs from the fatherland—all confirm our strong European ties. The town of Holland, Michigan, has become a luminous star on America's springtime radar screen.

The Ralph Kraal family's reception to their new homeland predated what we second, third, and now fourth generationals have come to love about springtime in Holland, Michigan.

The Ks had traveled by sea and finally by train from Ellis Island in New York. I wonder if the story of Abraham's family being called to leave the immorality of their birthplace weighed heavy as they considered the imminent struggles ahead.

The family arrived at the Grand Rapids train station on a cold November day in 1927, without fanfare and with two wide-eyed children in tow. They were met by distant cousins who had prayed for family to join them in the new country, but they came without sponsors.

These young American cousins were excited and expected to see *real* Dutch costumes and *real* wooden shoes. Seven-year-old Ali and five-year-old Jacob, however, knew nothing about wooden shoes. They were city kids, and wooden shoes were most often worn in rural areas.

The family came from the province of Overijssel and lived in the town of Almelo, where Grandpa managed a small grocery and staples store on Main Street. Their living quarters were behind the store and separated by a curtain. For reasons unknown, Dad (Jake) was born in Zwolle, but the family remained in Almelo, where Ali was born two years earlier.

When the tearful goodbyes had been said, there was no reason to believe they would ever see their Dutch relatives or the homeland again. This was the commonsense truth of T. S Eliot's words: "To make an end is to make a beginning." Grandma and Grandpa would have agreed, but they had yet to learn its implications in the uncharted life that lay ahead.

Grandma and Grandpa followed the path of Grandma's two other sisters (Gertrude and Johanna), who had come to America thirty years before, in the late 1890s. One sister's family lived in Grand Rapids and met them at the train station, but because of distance and lack of transportation (Grandpa and Grandma never owned a car), the families were unable to connect very often.

In Holland, the family found a cheap rental to share with Uncle John and Aunt Seine, Grandma's remaining sister, who had immigrated with them. They had no children but happily shared their life with Ali and Jake, considering them an important part of their own family.

Once Grandpa got his bike, he drove it everywhere, as he had done in the homeland. Grandma walked to church and the grocery store, and the children walked or biked everywhere they went.

The children were immediately enrolled in Christian school and pretty much left to fight their own battles—everyone learning a foreign language and the peculiar ways of the New World, their clothes and haircuts marking them clearly as misfits.

English as a Second Language (ESL) programs, required today, were not available to them or their teachers, who ofttimes had only an eighth-grade education themselves. They would have had limited knowledge or tools to help foreign-born children overcome the language barrier or deal with related issues. Sadly, both children retained painful memories of those initiation days.

Very soon after they arrived, clouds of the Depression (1929–1939) threatened America and beyond. With minimal English skills, Grandpa was forced to take a menial position with a furniture factory until he got a job cleaning ovens at the National Biscuit Company, to support his family. He remained a loyal worker until his retirement.

The Depression years took a heavy toll on immigrants who couldn't speak the language well, and Grandma and Grandpa were no exception. They lived in a number of small rental houses before they were able to purchase the house I remember best as a little girl, located on Sixteenth Street in downtown Holland.

Grandma was a stereotypical Dutch lady. Wherever she lived, the place took on a spick-and-span *godliness*. She would take a rundown rental, scrub and paint, hang new curtains, and add flowers inside and out. You can be sure it was more about elbow grease than dollars spent.

Sadly, the landlord would seize the opportunity of their upgrade to raise the rent, and Grandpa and Grandma would be on the move again.

During one of the frequent moves "from one corner of town to the next," Aunt Ali remembers pulling a neighbor's wagon filled with boxes of family photos. She was fighting a heavy wind when the wagon capsized, and sadly, a number of photos were lost. She has many memories of moving days, but most were not happy.

Grandpa and the two children learned English quickly on the job and in school. This helped to alleviate their differences. Grandma Kraal had been in America nearly twenty years by the time I came on the scene, but never having worked outside the home, she never fully adopted the English language as her own. When Grandma talked, we would get a sense of whether the answer should be a yea or a nay, but much of the time we just shook our head or said uh-huh or uh-uh. I learned to listen well and respond according to her facial expressions—always persuasive and visually effective.

My memories go back to the squeaky clean smells and Dutch lace curtains fluttering in the breeze and the beautiful flower beds that were so beautifully maintained.

Later in life Grandma and Grandpa built a two-bedroom bungalow on the west side of town. I remember a price tag of ten thousand dollars. Over time, Grandma and Grandpa, experiencing the wisdom of their decision to follow God's direction for their family, had been blessed to provide a comfortable and secure life for themselves and their children in this new town and new country.

Something to Ponder

> What would you see as the biggest obstacles in coming to a foreign land where no one understands your language?

> If you have immigrant ancestors, do you appreciate the courage it took for them to leave a beloved homeland, often with small children in their care, to come to a place they knew next to nothing about?

> Are you thankful for the gift of freedom and the blessings you enjoy because of the price your ancestors paid to build a better life for their family?

Two Scoops of Sugar

Therefore, since we are surrounded by so great
a cloud of witnesses, let us also lay aside every
weight ... and let us run with perseverance ... looking to
Jesus, the pioneer and perfecter of our faith ....
—Hebrews 12:1–2 (NRSV)

When I was very young and our family was still small, Sunday was the only time we had dinner (not lunch or supper). Sometimes, we were invited to Grandma and Grandpa K's—for Sunday dinner. I remember being very excited and hurrying my little legs up the stairs, where Grandpa would be waiting at the open door.

Grandma would be in the kitchen, always stirring something on the stove, and it smelled wonderful! She wore a clean flowered apron covering her mid-calf length Sunday house dress, accented with timeworn house slippers on her feet.

She was a very good cook, in the Dutch tradition. Cinnamon, nutmeg, and plenty of salt were mainstay spices in her kitchen, and let's not forget sugar! Lots of sugar, particularly in the applesauce. And, don't forget—two heaping teaspoons in a pretty and petite cup of hot tea. That was the norm. Grandma was not one to bake much, but she loved the local bakeries. And we loved bakery goodies.

Something tells me that Mom, in her own farm-girl tradition, might have contributed several loaves of homemade bread and butter and maybe her eight-egg Sunshine Cake for dessert. Baking was much more a part of Mom's life than Grandma K's, but Grandma might have held the edge on the stovetop.

The smell of savory pot roast; dark, smooth, and creamy gravy; chunks of hand-mashed potatoes; and spinach cooked in milk, butter, and nutmeg, sprinkled with lots of rusk crumbs, can transport me back in time in a flash.

Fresh, hot applesauce was a staple on Grandma K's Dutch

dinner table, and Dad's plate was incomplete without applesauce hand-whipped into his mashed potatoes and gravy. Cauliflower or brussels sprouts tasted best when buried in a cream sauce. Mom, on Dad's behalf, carried these traditions from Grandma K's table to ours.

It's hard to imagine what dinner at Grandma K's meant for Mom. She had cooked and cleaned for a crowd of hungry farmhands up and until she married, and now, her own young family demanded her every waking moment—in the kitchen, the garden, or the henhouse. Let's not forget the ironing board or the sewing machine, or headed out the door for a night shift to pay for tuition. How nice it must have been to sit and simply enjoy.

We loved spending Sunday afternoons in Grandma's and Grandpa's beautiful yard, but roughhousing was *verboten*. My mind's eye always catches a glimpse of the shiny glass globe and the welcoming birdbath. For the birds, that is. We weren't allowed to touch either one. And windows—why does every child have to touch the windows?

My job, oldest of the eight, was to prevent any child from misbehaving or touching those spotless windows or outdoor sparklies.

One of Grandma and Grandpa K's concerns for our big family was that Mom and Dad wouldn't be able to provide for so many children. As a struggling immigrant family, they could look back on the hardships of WWI and the Depression years, which enveloped the country shortly after their arrival. But God blessed our family in the same way He had provided for Grandma and Grandpa when they chose to pack up their little ones for the long and dangerous voyage to a land unknown and so far away.

We always had enough—enough food and clothing, overall good health, blessings and grace for the difficulties and the stresses of life.

Grandma and Grandpa K's eleven grandchildren raised their own families to love and serve the Lord as they were taught. And the promise, *to the third and fourth generation*, is now being carried forward into today's world.

A cup of tea and two scoops of sugar … celebrating you, Grandma and Grandpa!

Something to Ponder

> ➤ What memories trigger the excitement, sounds, and smells of childhood?
> ➤ What happy memory could prime the pump for pleasant conversations around your own family dinner table? If you are alone, find a sunny spot to sit and conjure up some sights and smells and tastes that you remember, and give thanks for the blessings of this day.
> ➤ Concentrate on one blessing your grandparents or parents passed along that has value for you and yours today. Thank God for their life and your own.

Men and Boys

Be patient ... See how the farmer waits for the precious fruit ....
—James 5:7 (ESV)

When I was very young, we lived just a short distance from Grandma B's busy farmhouse where Mom grew up. I spent many hours around the table with uncles and aunts. I remember discussions about the weather, if and when to plant or harvest, too much rain or not enough, and what could or must be done yet—today! Somewhere between ten and fifteen mouths and minds, with twenty to thirty work-worn hands and the same number of smelly stockinged feet, might have circled that beat-up, long and lean old table.

It was a simple but strong Christian family who recognized their complete dependence on God's favor—for the crops in the field—and health, safety, and security for all. God was central and rarely forgotten.

Awakened with the rooster's crow, everyone kept moving on through to the supper hour and beyond.

I remember the scuffle of chairs as Grandma's boys left the table and headed out the door. That would have followed Grandpa's reading of a lengthy Bible passage as we snaked slowly and methodically from the Old on through the New Testament. The silk ribbon bookmark determined where the next meal's reading would begin. A second and final prayer signaled everyone back to finish the uncompleted work of the day.

No secret where the guys were headed. Possibly to finish the chores in the darkness of a blustery winter night with snow three feet deep and rising. Maybe it was a soggy field where brawny manpower was required to heave-ho one or two marooned tractors out of a muddy quagmire. Wherever the need was urgent, there the boys and possibly one or more hearty sisters and (eventually) grandkids converged.

No one complained of being bored, and lazybones found no retreat on this farm. Seasonal change brought a variety of different tasks, but the work was never done.

Fixing multifarious farm equipment, sinewy six-foot-plus adolescents became excellent mechanics. They learned how to plant the seed and how to harvest the crops. They learned management skills, book keeping, and animal husbandry while on their journey toward manhood. On Grandpa's farm, boys learned early on how to become men.

It must have been more difficult, but Grandma managed to find quality mother-son time as well as mother-daughter time. For conscientious "tuff-stuff" farm boys, food and lots of it was a vital part of one's well-being. Fortunately, they knew the chief cook and bottle washer personally. Her love and guidance were woven into the coveralls of their hearts like the endless patches on their jeans.

My two brothers eagerly followed in the muddy footsteps of their mentor uncles and Grandpa, taking on any task, tutored or untutored, with gusto. They also stayed close to and protective of our own mom. Their hearts were open to her approval and her advice, though not always their independent feet and minds.

Something to Ponder

➢ Name for yourself several growing up experiences that might not have been pleasant at the time, but in hindsight you see value in them.
➢ What were the best times of your young years, and what made them so memorable?
➢ How do Christian parents instill the Word into their children in today's world?
➢ In what direction does your heart lean—toward the "olden days" or toward life as it is for you today? Why?

Gardening for Real

> God Almighty first planted a garden.
> And, indeed, it is the purest of human pleasures.
> —Francis Bacon

Out of necessity and to my mother's delight, our family was deeply committed to serious gardening. Our miniature farm included ten acres of woods and creek to explore and fish. Nearly fifteen acres were devoted to cash crops and a large vegetable garden.

I knew early on that gardening would not hold a dominant place in my future. This kind of backbreaking activity was painful for me, even then. Our two acre field of human suffering, aka the pickle patch, and ten acres of field corn needing to be harvested manually, demanded a large portion of our summers and after-school hours late into the fall season.

Mom's crème de la crème, the crown jewel of the property, was the large family garden Dad cultivated and dragged out of that hard clay loam. It kept our family bountifully fed in summer and fueled us through the long Michigan winters.

We canned everything we could stuff in a jar: beef from Grandpa's butcher block, vegetables and fruits, and lots of sweet, dill, and bread-and-butter pickles. Strawberry jam on Mom's homemade bread was a sweet treat for us, especially knowing where it came from.

I can only imagine the delight of housewives everywhere when freezers took center stage in basements or on back porches. Freezers would change the lives of women, particularly farm women, forever—and for the better!

Today, gardening is often done for the simple pleasure of watching tiny sprouts grow into strong plants and finally being able to enjoy the fruits of your own effort.

Fresh, local markets are great, but there's nothing better than going to the backyard to pick tomatoes, beans, peas, or corn and maybe some fresh flowers for the table—just before dinner.

This is gardening—for real!

Something to Ponder

> What gardening memories (if any) bring about pleasant thoughts?
> What makes getting your hands dirty worth the effort?
> Is there a comparison you can draw between gardening and your life?

Bringing Home the Bacon

> Sometimes you struggle so hard to feed your family
> one way, you forget to feed them the other way—with
> spiritual nourishment. Everybody needs that.
> —James Brown (American musician)

Several theories exist about where the phrase *bringing home the bacon* originated. A legend from the eleven hundreds refers to the church awarding a side of pig to the man who could honestly say he had not fought or even argued with his wife for a year and a day. No results are given. In the sport of boxing, the winner was the one to bring home the bacon in the form of a trophy.

On the American farm scene, it all begins with slopping the pigs and piglets—mashing together kitchen scraps and available farm greens with an appropriate feed mixture and copious amounts of water. Ham, pork chops, and bacon are the end products after slaughtering, curing, and smoking. You could literally bring home the bacon.

Generally speaking, however, anyone who provides the necessities of life for his or her family is one who brings home the bacon.

A continuous feed belt and production line had to be maintained on Grandpa's farm for chickens, cows, horses, and assorted other foragers: cats, ducks, goats, turkeys, and sundry other useful and pesky scavengers. Gathering the hens' daily gifts usually fell to Grandma or one of the girls, as I recall, although I vaguely recollect seeing Grandpa bent over in the henhouse, scooping out eggs with his thick and calloused farmer hands from under a nesting chicken.

Awaiting the birth of calves, piglets, or horses meant an occasional sleepover in the barn for uncles and possibly aunts. That was the exciting life of a farm kid. Early days of spring and summer meant late nights plowing, cultivating, and then seeding acre after acre of corn, wheat, oats, or soybeans. Those furrows must have looked endless when ground was first broken.

Harvesttime might have been more fulfilling, but the task list was no shorter. Funny, but I rarely heard complaints. Grandma's bunch not only seemed to accept their lifestyle but were joyful in the life they were blessed to live and the fresh country air they breathed. I'm quite sure they slept like babies.

Bringing home the bacon, on this and any farm I know, meant getting the work done so you could feed your family and reap the rewards.

On a spiritual level, the precious fruits of Grandma's and Grandpa's labors are evidenced in the hearts and lives of their six boys and seven daughters, who grew up to love and serve the Lord, carrying out the mandate to teach and mentor their own families "in the Way."

Eighty plus years later, generations of greats and grands are scattered across this country and beyond, planting seeds in tiny hearts, nurturing and reaping precious fruits by reason of their own parenting and mentoring. We too will be "those who through faith and patience inherit the promises" (Hebrews 6:12 NRSV).

If our grandparents or parents were able to peer into our lives today, they would be amazed to discover the wide outreach of family members actively involved and living out their faith.

Something to Ponder

- ➤ What does *bringing home the bacon* conjure up in your own mind?
- ➤ What is special about the heritage of your own family?

Good Writers Are Good Readers

When I look back, I am so impressed again with the life-giving power of literature. If I were a young person today, trying to gain a sense of myself in the world, I would do that again by reading, just as I did when I was young.
—Maya Angelou

I learn many things from writing coaches, but this bit of advice no writer can ignore: *To be a good writer, you must be a good reader*— and that works for me.

Generally, I'll have five or six books of different genres going at the same time. I'm quite sure no one is interested in some of the books that keep this writer awake at night. Glancing at the current assortment of authors hanging around my reading chair, I can't help but smile—Dostoyevsky, Buechner, Bonhoeffer, Jonathan Cahn ... oh my!

A few days ago, a friend stopped over while I was writing. She sat down in my office—in that same chair. She looked around and, with a rather strange look on her face, said, "What is all this heavy-duty stuff you're reading?" I told her I was preparing for seminary. She thought I was serious. And crazy!

I embarrass myself remembering how excited I was to get the mail last week. Yea for Amazon Used Books! John Calvin's *Heart Aflame* was stuffed in the box with a bunch of Christmas cards.

Used. By whom? It's old (1999), but the binding has never been cracked. Maybe not as popular as I had hoped. Friends who suggested this book of *Daily Readings from John Calvin on the Psalms* must be out on a limb—just like me, I muse.

Then I read the first lines of the Foreword by S. B. Ferguson: "You may have mixed feelings about a book of daily readings from John Calvin's writings. His name is not the first that comes to mind for most Christians ...."

My point, exactly!

Ferguson justifies his work by suggesting, "We use books like this one to 'prime the pump spiritually.'" Oh, I like that.

After reading several essays, I'm in total agreement with his assessment: "I suspect that you will experience a delightful surprise" because JC was one who discovered his own experience mirrored in the Psalms to be a "mineral-rich quarry of theology" (pg. v).

Voilà! I'm there.

***

"John Calvin?" says one of my five sisters, at a rare luncheon, just a few hours later.

"It's a devotional on the Psalms," I say. She doesn't ask any more questions.

I need something of historical significance for today's messed-up world, I say, not out loud. *Biographies and autobiographies should inspire us to greater service and contribute toward improving ourselves and society.* Blah, blah, blah, Anita!

I bore myself trying to explain why I read what I do. Sometimes I can hardly believe I'm talking about myself. Rare birds are hard to find, but I just might be one!

Something to Ponder

- ➤ What genres of literature interest you most?
- ➤ Does your reading menu challenge you to grow as a person?
- ➤ Does what you read inspire and initiate growth in your spiritual life?

Misfit Writers

I've just been invited along for a ladies' outing with some old
school friends for an all-day shopping trip. We'll be stopping for
a nice breakfast. Lunch will be special, and my friends and I are
excited.

Then my mind starts racing. What will I do when we start
circling the same sales aisle for the third time? What if they want
to go to one more junk store, and I already have a bothersome back
screaming, *Sit down ... now!?*

It's then I remember that my editors are getting antsy for The
Manuscript—already eight months overdue, in my mind. And
I'm considering shopping? Pretending I have nothing better to do?

Shopping has always been more of an inconvenience than a
fun event for me, but I would hate to miss the camaraderie, and
even worse, breakfast and lunch with the girls. I hate to think I'm
a misfit, but it sure feels like I am. They may never ask me again.

Finally, not able to commit or deal with my overly conscientious
conscience, I offer a simple platitude: "I'm really, really sorry, but I
just have too much on my plate right now. Promise you'll ask me
next time?" I'm sad.

"We'll miss you!" they say. I hope.

Are all writers misfits? Susan Sontag, speaking of writing,
acknowledges what I feel in this weak-kneed state: "There is a
great deal that has to be given up or taken away from you if you
are going to succeed in writing a body of work."

Now that does not sound appealing. But then, though I know
I will have to give up "a great deal," I also know there is reward

for the one who perseveres. I struggle now, as I have in the past, but in my heart, I know the One who walks every mile with me and is the Light I follow, through dark tunnels and then on into the bright sunshine.

Candice Millard, best-selling historical novelist, says it this way: "If uncovering the truth is the greatest challenge of nonfiction writing, it is also the greatest reward." Ticktock.

Staying up later than late, sneaking out of bed when I cannot put my swirling thoughts to sleep. It's a timeless concern and not at all new to my patient and tolerant spouse.

Tonight is one of those nights. I'm lying in bed, fitfully reworking words in my head that refuse to come together on the page. *Flat and uninspiring*, I mutter to myself. So I put on my robe and slippers and boot up my sleep-deprived computer, promising myself to be back in bed by midnight—my usual cutoff.

Midnight is now history, and so I retreat, not having accomplished what I attempted to do.

I'll come back in the morning, but for now I need some reassurance, and certainly redirection. I open the Word to Mark 4 where Jesus calms the storm with his voice: "Peace be still!" (vs. 39).

Very soon my heart quiets, and my disconnected and somewhat negative thoughts begin to unravel. In my renewed mental state I shuffle off to bed, relaxed and peaceful.

Next morning, opening up with yesterday's mind-bender, I wonder what all the mental angst was about.

Something to Ponder

➤ What is it that makes you stand apart from others in your circle or circles?
➤ So are you, like me, asking: *Why ... why ... why, do I do what I do, knowing what it will take to reach my goal? And what is it that I really do want to accomplish?*

➤ Expect the road to be littered with broken dreams. It takes a lot of compost to create a fertile garden. Remember those broken dreams? They produce an organic fertilizer that makes for a good compost heap. You can use it generously. Just keep adding value to what you do.

➤ Go ahead and chase a dream. Do something that truly inspires you. And don't apologize!

Sisters

A sister is a gift to the heart, a friend to the spirit,
a golden thread to the meaning of life.
—Isadora James

It's early in the morning—too early—but my brain refuses to settle back. It flits and floats from here to there, but then it settles gracefully on one of my favorites topics.

Sisters. I'm going to have lunch with sisters today! And when we meet, there will be hugs and kisses all around.

Before the next ticktock, my legs propel me out of bed. Before I brush my teeth, I know exactly what I have to do this morning. This very morning. I meant to do this a long time ago, but something always holds me back.

I'll pour a fresh cup of Vanilla Bean Crème Brûlée, smooth and silky, for this special day.

My office is dark, but the computer lights up, so I open to New Document. The title comes easily: "Sisters." My heart skips a beat, and a smile comes to start my day.

Then, almost immediately, I feel the panic rise from deep inside—and it's not the first time. I refuse to be deterred, but the ready defense on my tongue quickly unnerves my fingertips. It's always the same: *Where do I start? So much subject material ...I could write a book! ...Please, not another one, Lord!*

The K sisters are a formidable bunch, it's true. I hear this from others who know us. By the numbers certainly, but then I think, it's really more about the energy projected in a room. We're like the wind: where it comes from, nobody knows, but there it is for all to experience.

Husbands, kids, and now our grandkids, would agree: "The aunts are The Aunts," and they all know, "The Aunts rule!" No one of us is overly domineering, but together, we are quite the force of nature in the family circle.

I have five sisters and a sister-in-law—she's been in the family nearly as long as the youngest of us and is just as single-minded to meet us at Anna's House. An even rarer occasion is when our sister from Canada comes to town. We'll all be there.

I have sisters. Yeah for me. And thank You so much, Lord!

Now, it occurs to me (since this brunch was a spur-of-the-moment decision) that planning in advance doesn't necessarily mean better attendance. These hastily pulled-together brunches have certainly rewarded our efforts. We appreciate that each of us is willing to drop what is droppable, and when it works, we're ecstatic. There will be six of us at Anna's today. Choosing a really good brunch spot also seems to make a difference in the numbers.

It mystifies me, For years now, I've waited for that magical burst of inspiration to write the perfect essay about *sisters*. Specifically, my own talented and graciously beautiful sisters!

Truth is, I have been inspired. Many times. Until today, I have simply settled the urge back into its tidy little box for another time and place. Too unmanageable, too precious, too unwieldy to tackle, I tell *moi*.

So then, today, *tackle* being the perfect word, I will *undertake*, *embark upon*, or *wrestle with* finding ways to say what's in my heart.

I suspect my biggest fear is that I'll fall prey to a wrestling match with the keyboard—what should or should I not include, where do I start, and where do I stop?

Each sister is loved and personally unique, in decidedly different ways. Each is a beautiful expression of goodness, affection, and God's grace. Each one is loved and honored by their children and husbands—a credit to Dad and Mom, who modeled sacrificial love as parents and were faithful to each other for a lifetime.

One thing for sure: these special women, each of us at one time or another, have faced hard-fought battles of the mind and spirit and learned to face life's most awful storms head-on—but no one of us has ever been truly alone, without family, or a heavenly Father.

As we grow older together, we take note that God has been immeasurably good to us, and we cherish our personal and shared memories. Those difficult experiences, some too personal to share outside the group, are the building blocks of the fine-tuned character we observe in each other.

Someone mused that, in heaven, we will have eternity to share stories. That's good news for writers who know full well, there are more chronicles deserving to be penned than a lifetime can produce.

To have a sister or sisters—and let's include our *sisters of the heart*—is one of God's bountiful gifts. This kind of sister is always ready to share the bright spots of our life but also willing to walk the plank with us, in the middle of a chaotic, out-of-control day or completely broken down by the side of the road.

These sisters—of the same or different mothers, intuitively find ways to help us refocus on what matters instead of the imaginary battles of our own assembly.

Sisters like mine have a way of lending another pair of eyes and hands to an untidy room or state of mind.

Together, we've turned many work-bees into impromptu lunch dates. We know how to lighten the load for each other, and we know how to start the party early when one of us kills the fatted calf.

The memories birthed on these special occasions precipitate some of our best stories and photograph albums.

***

The two oldest of our band of six were married in a double wedding, now fifty years ago. As you might expect, there is an inside edition of this story. By pure coincidence, the original dates chosen were within three weeks of each other.

A tearful and painful decision surfaced after much sisterly warfare and high-pitched discussion with girlfriends—unfortunate enough to be our roommates and dragged into a mediation process. It finally ended in a simmering acquiescence to reason and the reality of economics.

Think of the logistics of getting a family of ten dressed and prepped for two weddings—one following on the heels of the other. By joining forces, we only needed two bridal gowns, six bridesmaids' dresses, two flower girls' dresses, two ring bearers' suits, two little sister dresses, and one nice outfit (hat, dress, shoes, gloves, and jewelry) for Mom. And tux rental for Dad and the two teenage brothers. Stage flowers? Cut in half and then halved again—with an already small stage covered end to end with two complete wedding parties.

What seemed practical and doable was never really a choice. Judy and I, the two oldest, aimed to make it memorable.

Our friends and family witnessed a rare occasion, for certain. One dad, two brides, two wedding parties, two kneeling benches, three pastors, and two grooms—one American, one Canadian.

No one in the family was without a stand-up part. Except for Mom. As always, she gladly took a back seat when it came to anything *out front*. Her only duty that afternoon, with hands and feet still numbed from the ratcheting intensity of her beloved Singer sewing machine, was to stand with Dad when he (twice nice) answered the question, "Who gives this woman to this man?" Fortunately, Dad and Mom were very happy to add these gentlemen to the family circle.

It should be noted, Mom had sewn three or four of the bridesmaids' sky blue satin dresses, our baby sister's frilly white flower girl dress, the two little sister dresses, and a matching blue ring bearer suit.

I didn't wonder then (I do now) how a busy working mom, with five kids still at home, most of them in Christian school—how did she possibly accomplish what she had to do, in less than six months, following a busy Tulip Time, with neither of the brides home to help? I know the answer. Midnight oil, instant coffee—and WJBL 91.3 FM. Let's not forget *grace*. God's grace. She counted on it!

***

Mom was one of thirteen, and we grew up knowing and appreciating the sense of direction she felt from staying close to her six sisters and six sisters-in-law. These sisters and family were a lifeline to the world outside her door. It was God and family who kept her grounded when the storms of life tossed her about on high seas.

Since that double wedding date, the K sisters have celebrated each other's weddings, babies, and milestones of faith and life, loved ones gone on ahead, and the pain of living with unanswered questions and unanswered prayers.

We know each other's strong points and strongholds, and we grow stronger by sharing the journey with our *sister-friends*, moving always in the direction of, and on toward, the endless Light of heaven.

A thousand pages could be written, and from the stirrings of those pages ten thousand more. Thankfully, we have all eternity to walk together in love and sisterhood.

Something to Ponder

> Don't miss the blessing of sharing with a sister or someone special how she or he impacts or has impacted your life.

> Who, during the course of your life, has been like a true sister or friend to you? Thank God, and determine to fill the gap for someone who is in need of a *sister-friend*.

> Draw up a list of people, and send a handwritten note or a beautiful card to someone who deserves your thanks or encouragement. Be assured, whatever you choose to do will be valued.

➤ I regret not showing more gratitude to a mother who gave her all for God and family. Writing and sharing her stories is a way to redeem the past. Find a way to do this in your own life.

Music ... Soul-Food of the Universe

> Music gives soul to the universe,
> wings to the mind, flight to the imagination,
> and charm and gaiety to life and to everything.
> —attributed to Plato

When I found this little truth from history's bounty, I knew this man loved what I love in life. Reread it, and see if it resonates somewhere deep inside you.

Returning to Calvin as a music major in my very late thirties was an indescribable experience—a script I could never have assigned to any actor and a plan I have never suggested to anyone else. It was painful in many ways. My prior music training consisted of two years of piano lessons around the age of ten. It wasn't the best of situations, so it wasn't hard to tell myself I could learn better on my own.

I regret not being more disciplined and that no one insisted I discipline myself. My teacher would always play a good portion of the piece—enough for me to automatically transfer the timing and even some of the piece to memory, without really learning what I needed to learn. Music shorthand—not a good thing.

Dad was the first soloist I accompanied. His standing instructions were, "Play it the way I sing it! *Forget the book!*" So I did my own thing. I was usually bored with the music as written anyway. This was not helpful for my later musical pursuits, but it gave me a heart and love for expressing the music in unique ways.

Dad was good at following wherever I led. That was when we were at our best. We sang almost exclusively from the *Popular Favorites* series of praise and worship songs. As soon as a new volume hit the stand, I would be in line at Meyer Music.

At some point, Dad had taken pains to restain our big old upright—black with a white grain filler—a distinctive and showy look we were proud to own. It was my baby grand!

Looking up the definition of osmosis, I find an interesting description of how I learned to play piano and later organ: "Osmosis is the gradual, unconscious absorption of knowledge or ideas through continual exposure, rather than deliberate learning." Wow! There it is! I absorbed what was necessary for my own enjoyment. Thankfully, others enjoyed it with me.

However, there is a wide divide between being gifted in music and being able to teach what one has learned through years of disciplined study. I have always been grateful for the gift of good musical sense and the desire to learn on my own. I was born with these gifts, but there is no substitute for disciplined study with a master teacher. In the words of Chinese philosopher Lao Tzu, "He who knows himself is enlightened." The more I learned, the more I learned how little I actually knew.

For many years, parents would plead for me to teach piano, and eventually I did, but I always suggested someone more qualified and made sure parents knew we would not go beyond intermediate level. Still they would sweetly say, "I really just want him to play like you." *Yah, sure.*

By fifteen, I rode my bike to church, to practice the organ for services. I don't remember who actually sat with me or how often, but I assume someone showed me some stuff.

I asked Marge, a family friend who accompanied Dad on organ or piano when I or my sister Shar (a truly accomplished pianist and organist) couldn't. Marge did not remember teaching, but I assume she was the one who gave me a few hints, especially how to use the pedals! And all those buttons. What fun!

Marge and I played piano and organ together all during my teenage years and occasionally, my college years. Sunday night hymn sings were popular, and we thoroughly enjoyed working together.

About that time, I was asked to play the Hammond organ for the dinner hour at a nice restaurant not far from home. I was too young to drive, but Dad faithfully brought and picked me up.

Start at five, finish at eight. Ten dollars an hour and whatever I wanted for dinner on break. Popular songs, praise songs, movie hits (which I had never seen)—whatever customers requested. This kind of night life was great! Eeeasy money! (Definitely easier than waitressing, I soon learned.)

Well and good, until the owner made advances. Dad had foreseen this and indirectly warned me never to accept a ride home. Sad day, indeed. It was the end of a lucrative job, and I was betrayed by my first real employer.

Soon I would be out of the nest and (mostly) on my own, getting settled into the world of higher learning. Mom and Dad had given me wings to fly; now I needed to exercise them.

Something to Ponder

> What did your parents contribute to your sense of self that carries you forward today?
> What was the "iron that sharpens iron" from your past?
> What barriers have you been able to break through because you were tough enough to push through the fears, intimidation, lack of self-worth—whatever could have but did not hold you back?

Breaking Down the Barriers

> Age is an issue of mind over matter.
> If you don't mind, it doesn't matter.
> —Mark Twain

Nineteen eighty-six was a banner year, especially for women who hadn't had the opportunity to attend college or wanted go back for their degree. Now, it seemed to me, it was in the news every day. I had shed many hot tears when forced to leave Calvin in my late teens. Now our two girls were growing up, one in high school and one in middle. The timing was right—I wanted to go back for a music major.

Still, I floundered over the best way to present the idea to the guy who would undoubtedly foot the bill. Al has always been quite fearless when presented with a new business opportunity, so one Saturday morning, I approached him with a good investment to consider—me. After a few good test questions, he said, "Go for it!"

I was at the end of two years of intensive back treatments. Later it was called prolotherapy. With God's blessing, the dynamics of our family life would be forever changed, and I was ready to finish what had been interrupted long ago.

Not realizing that the growing statistics of women entering or returning to college were based on community and state-run colleges, I set up an appointment with a counselor at my beloved alma mater.

At thirty-nine, I was double the age of incoming freshmen. Some of them would become my classmates! I would be one of less than thirty students over the age of twenty-two—out of four thousand. Obviously, Calvin was church based and not yet leading the charge to throw out the welcome banner for older than average students—but they were eager to work with me.

Thank goodness, I was blissfully unaware. I would never have attempted to break this glass ceiling.

Music theory was my very first class, followed back-to-back by keyboarding and music appreciation. That first day, I felt as though I were drowning in a nine-foot pool of TMI. Too much information! I sobbed all the way home, my mind made up. I was never going back!

In my disheartened state, I was convinced that Dr. Topp, my music adviser, had oversold the program and just wanted a guinea pig for Calvin's fine arts/music program. *Let's take this newbie off the street and see what we can do with her.*

It should be no surprise that most college music majors are a concentrated group of serious highfliers and scholarship-blessed by the time they find their way to the college campus.

With no formal training beyond last year's piano lessons with a good teacher, I was the best of the best misfits in this heady world.

Dr. Topp called me at home after I failed to show up the next day. He gave me no sympathy and told me to meet him in his office in one hour. The rest, they say, is history.

Most of my professors were in my age range and determined to help the comeback kid, but it was an extremely difficult time for me. Until I decided. Yes, it was a conscious decision—to give up my fears, relax, smile, and be friendly with these young and determined classmates. After that day, we became a mutual support team.

One of my professors stopped me in the hall sometime later to share that he and my other professors thought of their odd prodigy as a "breath of fresh air" in the music program. Raising a hand to ask for clarification was rare in any of my classes. "We love how you get the class tuned in and turned on, asking questions the kids have but don't dare ask." Tears again.

Still, the devil on my shoulder kept harassing: *This is insane! Why work this hard? Life is just getting good, so enjoy it. Take care of your family. You love volunteering, and there are so many opportunities, Anita!*

None of what I earned and have today would be mine if I'd

succumbed to the negatives screaming inside my head for all those embattled years.

I requested a tutor early on, and Kevin became my best friend on campus. The son of teacher/musicians, Kevin had been exposed to classical piano, organ, voice, and more—"long before birth," he mused. His life was encapsulated by a continual feed of cultural events and music—particularly the classics, but his new love was jazz.

Jazz! Really? I never got into it.

Until our only grandson took up trumpet in middle school and fell head over heels in love with—jazz! Now he studies and performs with the jazz band at Western Michigan University. Go, Reese!

Who can tell where the tree will fall? We, Grandpa and I, are learning to love jazz—especially the trumpet solos.

I must have been a true study for Kevin, but he never missed a session and couldn't wait to fill in any background information to help me understand my past, present, and future assignments. He was a godsend! With his help, someone with very little formal training achieved a music major within the normal time frame and a GPA to be proud of.

I'm sure he teaches differently today because he had to learn how to back up to a starting point he had never known.

Remember hearing, *You can't teach an old dog new tricks?* I did have to work very hard—like a dog, they say, but I proved them (and myself) wrong. We are all teachable, if we choose to believe in the power of prayer, hold fast to faith in God and oneself, and be humble enough to accept help. And then we must decide. What is it we really want, and are we willing to go to the mat in order to win what we have fought for so hard and so long?

My two-year music major was completed in the normal four semesters—three courses each, an internship in elementary and middle school, two full years of classical piano lessons, two summer courses, and an interim study of Amadeus Mozart—culminating in a skittery Calvin van, headed for a weekend in Chicago. Five young academic highfliers, our professor, and me—on our way to attend the play *Amadeus*. Mozart, that is. Who could have predicted, two years before?

We had come to know each other well in those two stressful years, each of us with strengths and foibles, hopes and dreams. Later that very special night, we shared our stories and shed a few tears together. And we laughed—I'm sure, too loudly. The successes we had earned were worth every painful effort. We were winners, all.

Unforgettable times in many ways. And daunting. I had to fight demons of self-doubt at every turn, but I had learned to enjoy music from a new perspective and with a greater level of understanding and appreciation. With perseverance and discipline, I had actually enjoyed performing a recital piece in the beautiful Fine Arts Center.

I had learned to love college life again. I had the confidence needed to complete my education major. I had no idea then that another two years would bring me to the starting line of the next leg of the journey—teaching music part time, all while headed in the direction of a master's degree in learning disabilities.

***

Nearly thirty years later, Dr. Topp and I met at a Calvin luncheon. We were seated at the same elegant table. When we introduced ourselves, I asked if he remembered me. He struggled for a moment but then said, "Anita! Yes, I do remember! I remember you by the sound of your voice."

He knew exactly where I had traveled in my teaching career: "Music at Potter's House, then you came back for a master's in learning disabilities—from Calvin!" he said, with a big, wide grin. He knew I had taught first at Potter's House and ended up in the school system where we raised our girls—starting at CC Middle and moving on to set up the Academic Resource Program at CCH. "You worked in tandem with the Christian Learning Center," he said.

"Yes, I taught there for nearly fifteen years."

"Aren't you glad you didn't quit that first day?" Instant tears, his and mine, told the truth. Today, I live with no regrets because of all those who helped me persist when the load became unmanageable.

Amazing how teachers remember those they have mentored, where they've invested so much of themselves! Now I understand exactly how that happens. The heart holds on to those who have made the deepest inroads.

There are students who can still make me smile. I could tell you something special about each one. When their name or face comes to mind, I say a little prayer for God to go with them, wherever they may be on their own journey. Now and then we meet, and joy comes back to visit.

It was very special to be able to thank this man, once again, for believing in me and encouraging me all along the way. What would my life be had I given up before starting this journey of a lifetime?

Michael Jordan says it well: "Obstacles don't have to stop you. If you run into a wall, don't turn around and give up. Figure out how to climb it, go through it, or work around it."

Amen, Michael!

Something to Ponder

> Think about someone who helped you become who you are today. Write a note or find a way to say thank you.
> Share with your family a piece of your history that shaped you into the person you are. Encourage them to do the same.

It's the Little Things

The kingdom of heaven is like a mustard seed ... It is the smallest
of all the seeds, but when it has grown, it ... becomes a tree ....
—Matthew 13:31–32 (NRSV)

Gardening could hold Mom's attention for hours on end. She loved
her vegetable and flower gardens. The cares of the world would
disappear when she left that busy kitchen with its never-ending
food-service line.

Judy remembers driving some distance to get strawberry
runners from a farmer. They had to be strong to make it in their
new clay beds. She also remembers packing them in thick blankets
of straw and watering them frequently. I remember a very long
hose that served to water the strawberries and other vegetables.
Of course, we also used it to cool down in the heat of summer.

Several varieties followed, but late in May, we would watch
for "Early Junes". Early June, early delight! Think—strawberries
layered on homemade bread, with homemade butter. Better yet,
homemade ice cream topped with sliced, sugared strawberries.

Sugar and snap peas followed soon after, and then it all began!

Summertime meals often consisted of one big pot of beans,
corn, peas, or whatever was ready to harvest. An acre of corn was
enough for all we could eat. I know our city cousins were always
welcome to come and pick corn and beans and other vegetables.

We sold corn by the dozens in city neighborhoods near Uncle
John and Aunt Seine and Grandpa and Grandma K. We'd drive up
in our beautiful (I thought) white Chrysler station wagon with red
top—the one I remember best. This would be timed with moms
wondering what to fix for supper. *Beep! Beep!* That was all it took.
City ladies knew the sound of fresh veggies, and soon we would be
headed home, probably with grocery money for Mom.

I remember it was more about sharing the bounty than making
money. It was a great experience for us and a good memory for me.

Late in July we started picking pickles—this, following many weeks of weeding and hoeing. None of us, except for Mom, were eager for those days. For the younger ones, *big* was definitely better. Mom knew the tiny ones they skipped over would earn much more at the loading dock.

Every day, we would beg her to quit and to stop following behind us! She only retreated when she had secondhand picked every row. We wondered why she hardly ever emptied her pail. We would say, "It's because you talk too much, Mom!" And that she did. She also knew, ten pounds of teeny-tinies was worth more than a hundred pounds of big cukes.

Today, when I buy pickles—sweets or dills—I think of Mom. The tiny ones are best. You know, it's true. It's the little things that count—that matter!

Something to Ponder

➤ Hmmm ... So, why are great big dill pickles, or cukes, not cheaper than prize baby sweet pickles on your grocer's shelves?
➤ What are the little things from your childhood that stand out as the best of memories?
➤ Go and make some memories today!

Harvest Time

A SONG of the good green grass!
A song no more of the city streets;
A song of farms—a song of the soil of fields.
A song with the smell of sun-dried hay,
where the nimble pitchers handle the pitch-fork;
A song tasting of new wheat, and of fresh-husked maize.
—Walt Whitman, "A Carol of Harvest for 1867," *Leaves of Grass*

Canning for winter storehousing was a necessity to extend a large family's budget, but it also meant we ate well and stayed healthy year-round. The process often began after supper, concurrent with kitchen cleanup.

Canning, whether by pressure cooker or hot water bath, superseded most other activities during the fall season, often cutting deep into the night. Those helping would slowly drift on up to bed, but Mom would be there till the last canner was unloaded. After cleanup, but while that last canner load burbled on, she probably grabbed *The Banner* or maybe the *Sentinel* for a few quiet moments of reading relaxation. I would often be there, sitting at the kitchen table, studying.

We canned beef when the milk cow needed a replacement or when Grandpa butchered. Every vegetable that would grow in our hard-packed but fertile clay soil was processed and canned or stored in the fruit cellar. When some of her eight kids had grown up, Mom acquired a big chest freezer. Things got a little easier, but canning was always best for things like tomatoes, peaches and pears, pickles, applesauce, beets, cherries, and, oh yes, strawberry and peach jam!

We even made a cinnamon apple butter from boiling the peeled skins and straining the mess through a colander, just like applesauce. It was wonderful! We did the same with peach skins. Mom knew it was a way to extend the family larder. She also knew that it's the little things we mothers do that help make ends meet while bringing enjoyment to your brood at the same time.

Mom determined that transparent apples were best for applesauce, and I would agree. They were available already in July and a family favorite. Of course, we canned applesauce from what we picked in Grandpa's apple orchard as well as any other reasonable or free source.

My mind skips over a few decades and I remember those memorable times with our own family of four, traipsing through orchards all around West Michigan. We had been told and we believed that apples were sweeter if picked after the first frost. So we would be ready to go the very next Saturday morning. No apples compare to those Al and the girls climbed after, sometimes hampered by winter coats and mittens, with light snow filtering through the trees. If we were lucky, we would find warm apple cinnamon doughnuts at the end of the hunt.

**

We all remember the time Mom was headed down into our Michigan cellar with a large box of canned tomatoes. The musty, earthy smell is acrid in my mind as I write. With a few remaining steps to go, she tripped and fell headlong into a mulch of broken glass and tomatoes.

Upstairs the sounds were breath-stopping. Mom immediately knew she had a major problem but somehow made it up the stairs, crying and frantically trying to hold together a large V-shaped gash around her kneecap. She was literally covered with blood and tomato purée.

The details of getting her cleaned up and wrapped to go to Emergency escape me completely. I remember looking over her arms and legs trying to distinguish blood from tomatoes. We later learned she had nearly severed the main artery in her leg.

Recovery was a long and painful experience, but complaining

about her injuries was not Mom's modus operandi. I do remember her bemoaning all the lost jars and tomatoes and the crutches she was forced to use.

She was soon back to her busy fall routine (too soon, I'm sure), just thankful to be able to do what she was born to do, gardening and mothering. I didn't realize then how differently the story could have ended.

Something to Ponder

➤ What memories come to mind when you think of harvest time?
➤ "You pick" orchards are now quite popular. The trees are much smaller and safer. No need for a ladder, and the harvesting season starts much earlier. How do your memories of that time of year differ from those of your parents or grandparents?
➤ What do you enjoy most about the fall season today?

The Gift

Life is short, break the rules. Forgive quickly, kiss
slowly. LOVE TRULY. Laugh uncontrollably and never
regret anything that makes you smile.
—Mark Twain

One childhood Christmas, I unwrapped a hand-sized, bulky, but fragile gift. I remember red and white wrapping paper. It was not boxed, so the gift wrap was its only protection. I had no idea what it would be, but I sensed it was a rare gift as I gently tore the paper away.

Inside, I found a kerosene lantern, painted green. It was made with real glass and no more than four or five inches tall. I was about eleven and thrilled to get something so unusual. So fragile. So pretty. With my name on the package!

I couldn't wait to light it up. Mom had to tell me it was really just for show. Being the oldest of about five kids by that time, I'd view anything frivolous for Christmas or birthdays as unusual. Most likely, Mom found it on a sale table at Penney's or Sears as she zipped by on her way to buy socks and underwear.

Before the Christmas party was over, one of the little ones picked it up. And dropped it. The lantern shattered. It was all over.

I wanted so badly to cry, but instead I hugged and comforted the child, who probably loved it as much as I.

I remember sitting with my journal that night. I'm sure it was just a simple tablet. I poured out my heart over my tragic loss. Soon after, I was just fine and moved on.

Something to Ponder

> What was your best childhood gift ever? How long did it remain as a valued gift?

> What is your favorite line from Mark Twain's little vignette—the one that sparked this essay?

Simple Deeds

Let us believe that God is in all our simple
deeds and learn to find Him there.
—A. W. Tozer

I followed Dad on many occasions—from church to church, from prison ministry to city missions and a county poorhouse—all for the privilege of serving as his accompanist. Sometimes this was on weeknights but most often Sundays.

Mom, who never said no to phone requests, would round up whoever was willing and available, and we would go wherever we were commissioned. My younger sibs probably wouldn't remember when they started singing. They were babbling and clapping to the music before they could walk or talk.

By the time I turned twelve or thirteen, I had learned to play a handy little pump organ for the summer Sunday afternoon services held by the Holland churches at a large blueberry farm north of town. Migrants living in temporary housing next to the field became our willing audience.

The guys would set up a staging area, and I would begin the service with a prelude—most likely a new song from the latest *Favorites 1, 2,* or *3.* I doubt whether number 4 or 5 was available then.

Dad would introduce his family and our songs and then lead the singing. Pump, pump, pump as fast as you can—left foot, right foot, up, down, repeat, repeat … Do not stop pumping!

Acapella singing was never a favorite with the Kraal bunch.

I remember a booming microphone, hot sun, and super-sore leg muscles. After a simple message, we would smile and shake hands with all who came by to say, "Gracias!"

We would say, "Gracias! Thank-you for coming!"

Our contribution was simple and, as I remember, very much appreciated by these dear families who had so little. For us, it was a great lesson in thanks-living.

As I revisit these signature moments in time, I see them from quite a different perspective. We were second and third generation "Dutchies." Dad had rejected the language of his homeland for the privilege of assimilating as an American, first and always. He had legally changed his name from Jacob to Jack when he decided to join the army, choosing America as his stated homeland.

Today, Spanish is a popular second language, but the only second language we would acquire would be the Dutch idioms and slang our grandparents used—occasionally and for effect, never in conversation.

Forgive me for not remembering more of my high school Latin phrases, like the first verb declension we learned: love—*amo, amas, amat, amamus, amatis, amant*. (We learned the little song you can pick up on the Web.) Where have all the Latin students gone? Gone to Spanish, everyone. Then there was our counting ability—in German: *eins, zwei, drei, vier, fünf, sechs* (we all loved that one), … *ein hundert*.

Now, as I remember ministering to this Spanish audience, it soaks in that neither we nor they really understood each other. Our Spanish-speaking friends possibly understood us better than we did them. They had to deal with English on a regular basis —in our gas stations, grocery stores, and post offices, where they brought their letters or gifts to send to their families back home!

I wonder if we appreciated that it really was God who would bless our love offering and increase it for His glory.

Years later, we can assume, this particular ministry was a catalyst to prepare the Tulip City for a dramatic change of citizenry. The predominant Dutch face of the city merged with a more colorful visage as the Hispanic population stabilized and grew strong in the West Michigan area.

Today, the Dutch are one of many ethnic groups naming Holland as their hometown. Spanish immersion classes are definitely *in*. (*Uno, dos, tres, cuatro*, Cinco de Mayo—yea for the beautiful holiday, on the fifth of May! Or a happy hour special at the Cinco de Mayo pub, north of town.)

We always felt blessed when we drove back home to our old farmhouse; there we had good food on the table and more blessings than we ever remembered to be thankful for.

We also knew the K kids would be out there the next morning, in the same hot sun as our Latin friends. We'd all be "picking pickles", but thank God, we only had two acres!

Late in the afternoon, we would share the loading docks with our Spanish speaking cohorts.

> Skinny little blue-eyed-blondes,
> some curly, some straight,
> All except for dark haired Ruthie
> and afro-curly Bob,
> Sitting on the loading dock,
> swinging skinny white, but sunburned legs.
> All, so quiet.
> Completely overwhelmed—'twas true.
> Garish jabbering all around, in this "other world."
> We, the K kids, were the misfits, rare.

I watched Mom—eyeing the scale, as each bag was weighed, especially the bag with her tiny "baby sweets," gleaned while she followed the younger ones. She knew the truth—not just the verbiage—"It's the little things that count."

As we sat there, probably contemplating how these guys— we thought they were a foot or so shorter than our lanky Brink uncles—with their dark, sweat-soaked hair and muscular frames— how they could be so tan. And I wondered, how would they know if they were sunburned, like we always seemed to be?

Today, Spanish reigns as second language, and some of our third and fourth generation family members have become fluent or at least have a basic knowledge of the Spanish language.

***

A Sweet Little Story

I remember hearing that Dad was invited to join Billy Graham's crusade in its 1940s infancy, but he could not afford the volunteer position offered or the travel time and expense. He chose to marry instead, and his ministry—of simple deeds and simple songs well sung—would be carried out much closer to home, where he chose to make a good life with a good wife and eight of his favorite people.

Dad often sang tenor with "George Bev"—sitting next to the radio, of course. George Beverly Shea was usually first to solo many of the songs that Dad sang. George Bev had composed the music for "I'd Rather Have Jesus" and words and music for "The Wonder of It All", two of Dad's favorites.

As a family, we rarely missed the Billy Graham crusades, once we had a television, whether they were on tour in the States or traveling internationally. Dad would sit in his favorite TV chair and croon along.

George Beverly Shea left this earth at the ripe age of 104, nineteen years after Dad died. I can't help but wonder if the two have spent happy hours singing together. George's friend, Billy, is with the Lord now, having died just prior to editing this essay. He was ninety-nine years of age in 2018. Men of faith, all.

Something to Ponder

➤ Do you have childhood memories of serving the needy in your community with family members?

➤ How did this influence your life then and now, as you think of serving others?

➤ What are the simple deeds that come naturally to you? How have they blessed your life?

Keep the Ball Rolling

Put me to the test ...; see if I will not open the windows of
heaven for you and pour down ... an overflowing blessing.
—Malachi 3:10 (NRSV)

Twenty five years after Mom delivered me to a brand-new freshman
dorm on a brand-new campus, Al and I delivered our first daughter
to the very same dorm, along with dad's hand-built to order double
bunk bed. We were delighted to see the banner strung across the
road celebrating this anniversary.

Since I was nearing the finish line for my own graduation
(yes, it had taken me twenty-five years to complete), Alicia and
I occasionally crossed paths on Calvin's tree-lined campus. She
loved to yell, "Hey, Mom!"

I wasn't keen on that. "Just say, 'Hey, Anita!'" I would beg.

Like my parents, Al and I wondered how this additional
commitment would fit into our already tight budget, but Al was
blessed with moonlighting opportunities, and I began teaching
music part-time at Potter's House. All the while, I was earning
continuing education units (CEUs) in learning disabilities. One
graduate level class at a time. Chug, chug!

Amy would join us on campus in 1990, the same year we
opened the doors to the Academic Resource Program at CCH,
and the same year we bought our Green Lake cottage. Life was
incredibly busy, but we were full of thanks-living.

God's answer to our faith and our prayers was in the constancy
of good health and sideline design and engineering jobs Al was
able to contract, along with my part-time teaching stints. While
I was buried in homework and lesson plans, a happy workaholic
husband never wondered what to do with his time. He just kept
on a-rolling.

Nothing was easy, but with patience, determination, and
fortitude for the long haul, we can now look back as a couple, to

celebrate the many ways our lives were enriched—before, during, and after that twelve-year endurance run. Al loved to say he put three girls through college and one through grad school—all at the same time. He deserved to brag, we thought.

One unlikely blessing came by way of the many hours I had been forced to spend listening to and studying the classics (Mozart's Piano Concerto no. 20, *The Marriage of Figaro*, and *Amadeus*) late at night, early in the morning, or while attending a concert. My all-time favorite was Schubert's *"Trout"* quintet—the fourth and fifth movements.

Al, having played cornet in high school, had an innate appreciation for music as well, but we learned together to love the classics in a fresh and new way and happily attended the Grand Rapids Symphony for many years as a result of those growing experiences.

Something to Ponder

➤ Recall a time when you had no idea how God would meet your needs, but then He carried you through and provided in a way you could not have imagined.

➤ Can you name an unexpected blessing you now enjoy because of something you were forced to learn, or had no control over?

A Christian Writer's Crucible

The crucible is for silver, and the furnace is for gold,
but the Lord tests the heart.
—Proverbs 17:3 (NRSV)

Sooner or later, the ride of life gets bumpy. Road hazards. Potholes. You decide to take a different route, only to find yourself on a crazy detour—off and away into foreign territory. You have no idea how you got here or where you are. Now, you are totally lost and paralyzed with fear. There are broken dreams, broken promises. A long and painful recoup ahead.

When there really is nowhere to turn, the Master Guide patiently comes to reclaim His own. He lifts us up, sets us back on the straight and narrow, and says, "Do you love Me? If yes, will you please just follow My lead?"

We may not feel totally ready, but He knows what He asks of us when He says, "Stop with the excuses! Get on with it. Follow Me!"

Convicted, I must admit that a few of my excuses have become strongholds in my life, especially those related to publishing and marketing.

Current writers might think me foolish when I shy away from doing things they consider to be necessary steps for good marketing strategy. (If you knew me in real life, you would know: *This woman has problems just like me, only different!*)

Here's a few of my loudest worn-out rants: "I don't want to do Facebook; it slurps up too much time. I think blogging is for people with not enough to do. I don't want to travel to book signings; I'm too old. I just want to write; I don't like all the demands of publishing and promotions."

So now that I've established my whinings in black and white, it's quite obvious how silly and misdirected I am. Misdirected? Well, maaybee … okay then!

First, I will have to pray and work toward a change of heart and attitude, toward getting my work out in the public eye (yeah for social media!). Then I will learn how to use whatever technology is necessary to effectively share the gifts He has given. I might even have to hire a web manager and learn how to blog!

Stopping long enough to reflect, I recognize these social media tools are exactly those used to project the Message to the farthest corners of the globe. It's all part of the Mission!

Well … here I am, Lord. Convicted once again as I read Psalm 92— about the righteous flourishing like palm trees, continuing to grow, still producing fruit in old age, staying fresh and green—or, as the NRSV translates verse 14, "always green and full of sap."

Got that! Fresh and green, and full of sap. My dad would say, "Full of vim and vigor." Or was it "vim and vinegar"?

Something to Ponder

> ➢ Many people live with the remorse of not accomplishing what they set out to do earlier in life or perhaps having given in to life's pressures and followed a lesser goal. Is it ever too late to correct course?

> ➢ What tiny step can you take today to set you on a more direct course? Name your obstacles, and decide how you will overcome them one at a time. Don't forget, you have the Master Guide at your side.

> ➢ It's never too early or too late to think about the legacy you hope to leave behind. Take some time to sit with family members, and tell the stories that make your family laugh or cry. Do it together. Then write it down!

> ➢ Tell the stories of those who have gone on ahead, to remind each other of their significance in your family.

Be Still!

Be still, and know that I am God!
—Psalm 46:10 (NRSV)

I was on summer vacation from teaching in 1996 when we tore down our beloved canary yellow cottage on Green Lake and started digging the footings for our new home. During the nine-month building process, we rented an eight-hundred-square-foot cottage only a few blocks away, on Round Lake. No room for much of anything, so we lived simply, ate on paper plates, and entertained as simply as we lived.

While the meat was grilling, we could relax on the patio overlooking a quiet and serene lake, savoring the sights and sounds of a summer evening.

We spent many evenings working at the new house, but late at night we happily returned to our cozy Round Lake sanctuary. Our only dresser fit exactly in the petite-sized walk-in closet. With no room for a bed frame, our queen-size mattress lay on the bedroom floor, welcoming and cozy. We loved it.

God knew exactly what I needed that unforgettable summer. Walking to the building site one or more times a day was pure joy, as we anticipated becoming permanent residents. I learned to love my new neighborhood, the sights and sounds and the people who stopped to chat.

Up the hill and out of the way of work crew, I watched it all take shape, one floor at a time. From an old plastic lawn chair, pulled from the neighbor's trash, I sat for hours and took photos of every step of the process. I look back with fond memories at the photo albums of these rare moments in time.

Many prayers ascended from that old chair. Prayers for safety for the builders and for a husband who integrated so easily and eagerly into the world of construction.

This guy is by nature the hands-on type, but an unfulfilling factory job post high school sent him scurrying toward higher education. Engineering is his forte, but he finds great satisfaction in getting his big hands dirty.

I was starting to recover after all that had preceded this move—completing a master's degree and thesis during the chaos of major family upheavals, teaching full-time, with the additional stress of moving. Spiritually, this was my time to rebuild and retool.

Many battles of the mind were faced, fought, and mostly conquered in that silly old chair. I never thought to replace it till the building process was completed.

It was there on the hill that I learned to trust God again— and to *be still!* Amid family joys and family tragedies—a daughter taking on the role as new wife and mother to a four-year-old who had lost and desperately needed a mommy—there was much to be thankful for and many reasons to pray.

I delighted over each exciting step of the building process, from the cement work to the studs and heating runs placed in the cement floors, to the balcony and decks surrounding the house. As the third-floor skeleton took shape, it seemed as though the bones were reaching for the sky.

Several days later we climbed the temporary staircase and stood on an unfinished third-floor deck to watch the first of many magnificent sunsets. The next morning, before the work crew arrived, I took those stairs to capture on camera an equally splendid sunrise. I was humbled by the immensity of God's favor toward us.

I learned more about house building that summer than I could have imagined. It was my privilege to romanticize and while away the hours envisioning what it would be like to actually live here year round!

As time progressed, I knew I was becoming sturdier and more resilient on the inside. I was ready now and anxious to move on, stronger for the journey ahead. And yes, I was grateful that God had taken His despondent child aside, sat her down in a rickety old chair, and said, "Be still!"

Something to Ponder

➤ Name for yourself a time or times when God took you aside to learn about yourself and more about Him and His love for you.

Writing Obsession

But if a vocation is as much the work that chooses you
as the work you choose, then I knew from that time on
that my vocation was, for better or worse, to involve
the searching for, and treasuring, and telling of secrets,
which is what the real business of words is all about.
—Frederick Buechner, originally published in *The Sacred Journey*.

I read these words over and over again that first time. I struggled with the phrase, *telling of secrets*. Sounds dark and naughty. But Buechner, a "neurosurgeon" among word tinkerers, was speaking as a writer who, by nature, is in constant search mode to unearth, polish, and package up his treasure trove of uncovered word gleanings, with an anxious mind to dispense these *secrets* to the world.

Theological and thought-provoking, Buechner's practical applications speak directly to the heart. As a venerated Christian author, he uses his words more eloquently than I, and yet they match the thoughts of my heart as I ponder the fact that my pen can serve as the conduit to bring God's love to people everywhere.

Whether we're young or old, a soccer player with teammates who don't know the Lord or a retiree living next to an unsaved neighbor, God longs for each of us to tell others the secrets of His love for each of us. He wants us to be obsessed with things related to Him and excited to reach out to those not yet connected to Him by faith.

Like gold to the gold digger, writing can easily become an obsession. I know, because that obsession has found its way into my bloodstream.

I live my life in constant search mode. I'm on the alert for quotations of honorable men and women of Christianity's past. Writers who have spilled the deep thoughts and secrets of their hearts. Writers whose words have survived the passage of time and deserve to be shared once again.

I never understood the real truth about writers and never understood the inner working of a writer's brain. But now, I understand: writers write because—we are writers! It's not really a choice. We write late into the night or before the crack of dawn, when we're hungry or in pain, and when we should be vacuuming or making dessert for company coming.

For one who has stories circling round, gaining momentum in the dark recesses of memory and begging to be given a voice, writing can easily become a God-given obsession.

Take a look at the amazing apostle Paul! Writing from a jail cell or cast away and stranded on a lonely island, by God's design and direction, he left an unprecedented and amazing legacy. He wrote from his heart and by God's Spirit, wherever his soul-winning mission propelled or dumped him.

Paul never forgot his roots or his friends back home. He never forgot or neglected his ministry! He lived, strong of spirit, green and growing, till God called him home. His inspired letters traveled by snail mail, crisscrossing Roman roads to reach those who knew and loved him, who served the same Master and were eager to receive his words of encouragement or his lessons for energetic living in a dark world.

For the past two thousand years, an invaluable volume of Paul's inspired letters can be found in the most widely translated, most loved book ever written, and that, by a dissimilar band of people, connected by faith to the one true God.

Today, Paul's letters motivate us for outreach, and in times of personal difficulty, serve as the stimulant we need for our own wilted or thirsty lives.

Something to Ponder

> Let the cool breezes of fresh ideas unlock your mind to the endless opportunities calling your name. What is He calling you to do with your life? Your life as it is today?

> If you are confined to your bed, wheelchair, or rocking chair, become a prayer warrior for neighbors, people caring for you, church friends, and grandchildren. What a great gift that could be!

> If you are mobile, don't allow yourself excuses. Volunteering is most rewarding. You get to decide where and when.

Play Ball!

Success is how high you bounce when you hit bottom.
—General George S. Patton

General George S. Patton didn't have a trampoline, but he knew the feel of a good rebound when he spoke of winning and defeat.

Developing a competitive spirit is universally accepted as an essential tool for life. On and off the field, in the classroom, or on the job. Sinking that basketball, scoring a goal, smashing that volleyball or tennis ball into your opponent's court—is there anything better?

Our seven grandkids have all been involved in sports at very young ages. Nothing pushes and tugs harder at a parent's or grandparent's sensibilities than a little kid's drive to be the center of attention.

As we concentrate on sportsmanship and the joy of winning, we are also reliving the fun through a child's eyes. Soon enough, the game gets serious, and let's admit that then we are ready to share in the glory of winning.

We were blessed to be there! Screaming ourselves hoarse, clapping our hands raw. Bitter cold, nasty drizzle, oppressive heat, or hanging out in a sweaty and stagnant indoor soccer court—we know the highs of winning and the sour smell of defeat. To be truthful, when they're young, it can be more painful for us, the divested spectators. After the coaches' encouraging words and the postgame treats, the kids have already moved on.

Soon enough, they will learn what it means to fight to the finish for their team and to never, never give up! What they learn, they will take with them into other areas of life.

Sadly, Grandma's "Good job!" won't neutralize the effects of losing a game, a tournament, or a coveted spot on the school team. Our only task then will be to serve as salve on a wound.

Love you, child. Win or lose—you're the best.

Kids learn quickly enough that losing is for losers, and not wanting any part on that team, they'll pull themselves out of the drainpipe and start smarter next time. Once they're back on the winning streak, it isn't long before the specter of overconfidence seeks out and overcomes its impudent and sassy prey. And then round two begins.

Life itself teaches us good lessons along the way, but parents, by God's design, have a huge responsibility. How they process and react to wins and losses—their own and their child's—leaves a lasting impression.

How quickly we and our children recoup after a loss depends on what we've learned and whom we've learned to trust. As adults, it is even more important now.

Here's wise old King Solomon, who had to learn a thing or two himself: "Trust in the Lord with all your heart, and do not rely on your own insight. In all your ways acknowledge Him, and He will make straight your paths" (Proverbs 3:5–6 NRSV). It's the winner's secret path to the gold!

Something to Ponder

➤ In what area of your life, could you use a little more practice time?

➤ In your mind's eye, sit down at your own funeral service. Are you amazed at the impact your life has had on others?

➤ If we could listen in to our children or grandchildren as they talk heart to heart with their own children, would we recognize a worthy legacy of godly leadership in what we left behind? Will the values we instilled in our children still be a guiding force in their children's lives?

Love Letters from the Heart

> Recite [these commandments] to your children and talk about them when you are at home and when you are away, when you lie down and when you rise. Bind them as a sign on your hand, fix them as an emblem on your forehead, and write them on the doorposts of your house and your gates.
> —Deuteronomy 6:7–9 (NRSV)

Most of my grandchildren loved to write "letters"—little messages from the heart, even before they could read. These preschool scrawls are the best love notes a grandma, grandpa, or parent can receive. It tells us they already love words. Beautiful words. And best of all, they love us.

They stuff their childish offerings into an artfully hand-crafted, sticker-laden envelope and smoosh it all together with scotch tape. What fun they had. And what a joy to open and receive these precious gifts.

When our youngest visited, she would plaster Post-it note squiggles all over the refrigerator. She and I would stand back to admire "all my words and letters and pictures—just for you, Grandma!"

Those years are gone for us, so if you have little ones, savor and catch all the love letters you can grab.

Now and then we get to see writing projects of older grandkids that give us a hint of what goes on inside their heads, whether teen, tween, or running hard to catch up with the pack. I often ask for a verbal summary of the latest book they are reading. Answers can be quite impressive—and delightful confirmation that the joy of using words well has taken root in the fertile soil of the next generation. It becomes part of the legacy we are blessed to leave behind.

I pray that, with all their learning, they choose to seek wisdom first. That they will be firm believers who will look for the precious secrets found in the greatest book ever written and be able to tell the greatest story ever told, passed along now for more than two thousand years.

But soon enough the pummeling of words and incessant images, with the confusion of *unethical ethics*, wars with our minds, charges at breakneck speed to control our thoughts and hearts and time.

It should concern us all, parents and grandparents, pastors and teachers, and coaches. So I humbly pray we remain faithful Light bearers—bringing truth and hope to change our world, one word or deed at a time.

Something to Ponder

> What are your thoughts about the importance of your words, spoken or written, for those you love and those who share your world?
> Psalm 19:14 (NRSV) says, "Let the words of my mouth and the meditation of my heart be acceptable to you, O Lord." How does this verse impact your free time, your "me time"?

Enough Already!

How many lessons of faith would we lose if
there were no winter in our year?
—Thomas Wentworth Higginson, *April Days, 1861*

Over the radio, on TV, in the grocery store, wherever you go, the first thing you'll hear right now is *Enough already!*

I'm writing this on March 30, 2014. It is a balmy forty-five degrees late in the day, but we have been bundled tight in ski jackets, wool coats, gloves, boots, and scarves, since sometime in November. We are ready to leave our hibernation havens— survivors of a true Michigan winter.

Record snowfalls across the state and nation. Record days below zero. Wind chills that brought home many a discouraged skier or snowmobiler earlier than intended— some actually declaring a truce, echoing with the rest of us as we beg for mercy: *Enough already, Lord!*

Temperatures continue to rise, and we now stand at fifty degrees. The warmest we have experienced for many months.

It must be true! *If March comes in as a lion, it will go out as a lamb.*

We will remember this as the winter Al shoveled off our multiple flat roofs and decks—three times! I could watch from a third floor window as he shoveled off the large roof over the garage below. I made it my job to make sure he didn't fall off or have a heart attack—untended.

Many stories of power outages, icy roads, and school and church closings persisted, but here in Michigan where the cold winds and snow squalls kept us on alert almost every week, we suffered less than many in other states.

Friends were caught in a seventy-car pileup just outside Atlanta. They spent seventeen hours in a car without access to the common necessities of life. Any questions?

Fortunately for them, they stayed relatively warm, but one can only imagine the nightmarish predicament of so many weary travelers not knowing if or when the storm would end. As it happened, many abandoned their cars, which compounded the danger and the hassles for road crews when the weather cleared.

When we come to the end of ourselves and face the reality of not being in control—at least, of the weather—we have to admit, there are other things completely out of our control as well.

Fortunately, we know the Keeper of the stars, the winds, and the storms. He promises that there will never be a storm so fierce that He cannot halt it with His voice, in His time.

When the storms of life cannot be settled here on earth, by God's grace and in His time, we will find ourselves in a place indescribably better. A place we will gladly call home.

The book of Job gives us a magnificent speech where God responds directly to the questioning of Job and his friends. Read it for yourself, and be awed at the majesty and personhood of God. Here are a few of my favorite verses telling of His greatness in nature. God questions Job:

> Have you entered the storehouses of the snow
> or seen the storehouses of the hail,
> which I reserve for times of trouble,
> for days of war and battle?
> What is the way to the place where the lightning
> is dispersed,
> or the place where the east winds are scattered
> over the earth? ...
> Does the rain have a father?
> Who fathers the drops of dew? ...
> Who gives birth to the frost from the heavens
> when the waters become hard as stone,
> when the surface of the deep is frozen?
> (Job 38:22–24, 28–30 NIV)

Job's testimony is humbling when he finally replies: "Surely I spoke of things I did not understand, things too wonderful for me to know" (Job 42:3 NIV).

Something to Ponder

> What have you discovered about God and His faithfulness during an unwelcome winter season in your own life, a time when hope was distant and faith seemed futile?
> Can you relate to Job's response in Job 42:3?

A Rare and Poignant Christmas Memory

Consider it a sheer gift, friends, when tests and challenges come at
you from all sides. You know that under pressure, your faith-life is
forced into the open and shows its true colors. Let it do its work so
you become mature and well-developed, not deficient in any way.
—James 1:2–4 (MSG)

Like many of you, our large but close-knit family has been through
some pretty rough waters together and have learned to appreciate
the ways we've seen each other grow emotionally and spiritually.

The loss we experienced during the Thanksgiving and
Christmas season of 1994 played an important role in who we are
today and how we value life and the lives of others. It is precious
to ponder a journey that began nearly twenty-five years ago and
continues to this day.

***

Our family was slowly learning to accept the unthinkable, as
Dad K, seventy-two years young, was fast losing an unrelenting
battle with pancreatic cancer. We found ourselves in one of the
most horrific and challenging times our family had ever faced
together. Until cancer started its surreal inroads, Dad had no
noticeable gray hair and appeared fit and healthy.

Hospice was on call regarding medications and caregiving, but
we, Mom and family, were his ready attendants. My sister Carrie
lived closest and had become Dad's most reliant care-giver, besides
Mom. As fifth child of the eight, she is the elastic that holds the
big kids and the little kids together. She is party planner and ever-
ready worker bee, whenever family events take place. Naturally,
she served us all by serving Dad so well.

Late afternoons I would leave work, drive to Holland to spend the evening, and then find my bleary way back to Grandville late at night when things settled.

We treasured every moment with Dad and every word he spoke. Just as important, we were able to share with him what needed to be said and lavish on him the love he craved.

Dad made it his mission to bring peace and acceptance of God's will to each one of us. He asked for forgiveness, many times over, for not being the dad or the grandpa he wished he had been to his eight children and twenty-six grandchildren. His was a marvelous testimony of grace and acceptance of God's will in his life. We were all gifted with personal memories of relationship building.

***

Earlier that year, Al and I determined to host one last Thanksgiving dinner in our big rec-room, downstairs. We would be selling our home, tearing down a beloved cottage, and renting another while we built our next home—this time on Green Lake. We had it all planned.

I was teaching full time and continuing to work on my thesis for a master's in education and learning disabilities. Data covered the game table in the upstairs family room. Numbers and graphs, facts and figures.

I was so thankful to have this part of the project finished and planned to bring it all to a finale during Christmas break. But now I fretted—about Dad, and then about gathering everything up to free up space for games and food and family on Thanksgiving Day.

The greater Zuidema family numbered thirty people on that storybook snowy day. Our own hearts were heavy, and emotions hung just above the waves of reality. We were intentional about focusing on the many blessings we shared in our lives and homes. Too soon, an exceptionally good dinner was cleared away. Creamed turkey was slow-cooking in the Crock-Pot for supper. Holiday snacks lined the counter. Everyone was in relax mode and content.

Al and I had made an earlier decision to drive the twenty-five miles to Holland to spend a short time with Dad, while the others enjoyed a lazy Thanksgiving afternoon together. Alicia, my dad's firstborn granddaughter, decided to go with us "to see Grandpa— one more time." Big kid Jerry, her newlywed husband, opted to stay and play with the kids.

Around three o'clock, we bundled up and promised to be back soon.

Football was the afternoon choice for the men. They took over the family room upstairs, with TV and fireplace. Ladies chatted quietly in a sunny living room. The only youngsters, a nephew and niece, were absorbed in delight as they romped in the snow with Jerry before scurrying downstairs to roughhouse some more. Amy and her fiancé were there to share in the fun.

When we arrived in Holland, other family members were standing quietly around Dad's hospital bed settled into the TV/ sunroom. It had been his preferred place to read the *Sentinel*, relax, and enjoy his favorite sports. That pastime was now history. We were living day to day, hour by hour, watching him suffer in excruciating pain. As hard as it was to let him go, we were just as anxious for God to call him home, where he desperately longed to be.

We quietly wondered again if this might be our last visit and how long Dad would be able to respond—now mostly with his eyes. We grieved together that life was moving in a direction we did not welcome.

A few minutes into our visit, the phone rang. Someone jumped to answer the annoyance. The voice on the other end was shaken and asked for Al. He listened while his face lost all color. He hung up and tried to respond casually by saying that something had happened to Alicia's Jerry and we needed to leave right away. Panic struck for Alicia and me as we were rounded up and hurried out the door, knees knocking, bodies trembling.

Alicia and I huddled in the back seat, barely breathing, not knowing what to pray, so we just whispered, *Jesus, Jesus* .... Al drove silently to Butterworth Hospital, downtown Grand Rapids.

We arrived as the ambulance pulled up with our Jerry and traumatized daughter Amy. She had just shared a wild trip to the hospital with the big brother she had so briefly but thoroughly loved and enjoyed.

We, Jerry's family and ours, were hastily ushered to a private room. The gravity of the moment was not lost on us. After what seemed like hours, we were told nothing more could be done. Heart attack—at twenty-five! Thanksgiving Day, November 24, 1994.

***

Sometime later we learned, as we were leaving my parent's home, Dad suddenly tried to raise himself up to say clearly, "Jerry beat me to heaven!" No one knew then what lay ahead, but Dad, with one foot in heaven's door, was given spiritual awareness of an event that would forever mark this Thanksgiving/Christmas season and our family's history—on both sides.

Alicia and Jerry shared birthdays. Same day, two hours apart. They had joyfully shared four birthdays together, two of them as husband and wife, and were planning how to celebrate a second anniversary on December 4.

Family members at our home witnessed and experienced severe trauma but also the protection and awareness of the presence of God, when only He could calm the storm raging in each wounded heart. They left our home with great sadness and memories too complex to fully unravel until much later.

Back in another room and another town, my brothers, sisters, cousins, and mother had to process yet another tragedy unfolding as they watched Dad turn his face to the wall. He rarely spoke again but lingered on for several pain-wracked weeks, lovingly cared for by family.

***

Jerry, precious and only son of Rog and Janna Anderson, was a first responder/firefighter, so his "brothers" had lined the street to our home when the 911 call went out. With these brothers, we would plan a firefighter's funeral late into the next evening of a very long day. They were determined to honor a fallen comrade, husband, son, brother, family member, and true friend.

On a blustery and bitter cold day, the city of Cascade's flags flew at half-staff, heaving hard in the wind. The somber beauty and pageantry of a Christian firefighter's service seared its way into our hearts and the hearts of his friends, some without God in their lives.

Jerry stood six feet eight inches, but the true measure of a man is found in the way he lives his life in relation to God and others. We heard many stories from numerous people who loved and respected him—firefighters, friends, neighbors, church family, and our own families. Jerry Anderson was a giant among men and a true servant leader.

Our families, his and ours, soaked up each other's pain like sponges, bringing yet another level of grief and loss. At times, the tears refused to stop. Other times, the tears were stopped up by anger, questions unanswered, or the apparent injustice of it all.

Emotions—the highs and lows—they follow you wherever you go. Somehow, in the storm, we kept hold of faith. We knew God's hand was good. In all things, we knew, God is good.

I had no time now to be part of Dad's last days on earth. Life spun us around in a whirlwind of funeral preparation as we grieved and tried to help a daughter cope and do what she needed to do. Nothing could have prepared Alicia or our family for anything of this magnitude.

Tragedies like this serve as their own caustic and distasteful teachers, and the families they rake over have no time to plan and no time to pray for God's will to be reversed.

One of God's finest provisions for our family during this time was that our beloved home had not sold when we tested the market during the previous summer. We were grateful for this familiar comfort zone, where we could spend time with a very brave but hurting daughter, as she prepared for the uncharted road ahead.

We gathered, those first days, around a dining room table lined with cards, photos, mementos, and coffee, tea, and drink cups. Food magically appeared, and others kept the house tidy for the constant flow of caring friends and family.

God's presence did not leave us comfortless, and immediately following the never-to-be-forgotten funeral service, we all went back to work.

Sometimes it helps to put grief on a shelf for a little while. I remembered going back to work for a few hours, even before the funeral, to set things in order for staff and my students. As I heard the main door close behind me and walked toward my office-classroom, I consciously stepped away from the reality of two concurring events threatening my sanity. For just a little while.

In some small and transient way, I mentally closed the door to sadness and grief and opened the door to a world still turning on its axis, where the sun still shone. I took my first deep breath of crisp air in a long while, and my heart sang bits and pieces of Horatio Spafford's song, "It Is Well with My Soul." Dad loved and sang this song often and for many others: "When sorrows like sea billows roll ... though Satan should buffet ... it is well. It is well with my soul!"

I felt peace settling deep inside and knew those words were my special gift for the day ahead.

As almost everyone learns at one time or another, normal responsibilities of life can and do coexist with grief. It can be a blessing and not always in disguise. God's hurting children can truly experience His presence as He walks alongside or carries us—through dark tunnels or a pain-filled existence.

God's grace is the most amazing gift to the believer in times of trouble. Specific to all our needs and sufficient in all circumstances, it will meet us where we are, even if collapsed in utter despair.

Philippians 4:19 (NRSV) isn't just another worn, weary verse in a dusty Bible. It is there for us. Let's work it through carefully: "My God (is He mine? yours?) will *fully* (in every way) satisfy *every need of yours* (sorry, not our wants) *according to His riches in glory* (His abundant grace) *in Christ Jesus*." The promise is ours, for keeps, if we have claimed Jesus as Lord of our life.

Two and a half weeks after Jerry died, I found my way back to Dad's TV room turned hospital room. On his last day this side of tears, I stood at his bedside with sister Carrie, trying desperately to alleviate the agony from his wasted body if only for a moment. We prayed desperately for God to take him home. We stood on either side of him for over twelve hours while family members came and went. Only grace and prayer got us through that grim day.

In exhaustion, very late into the night, Carrie and I fell on the couches to spend what we knew would be Dad's final hours. In the stillness of night, we saw him being completely released from pain. Mom sat quietly by his bed as they silently shared the last hours of fifty years together, hand in hand.

At sunrise on Sunday morning, December 11, 1994, Dad peacefully went home to be with the Lord and all those gone ahead.

We felt blessed to know our Jerry would be one of those smiling faces welcoming him to his eternal home.

*(Completed on what would have been Dad's 91*st *birthday, November 9, 2013)*

Something to Ponder

> Are there painful events in your life that resurface after reading this essay?
> Be willing to let it go and claim the promise of Philippians 4:19. Then thank God for guiding you safely through the storms past and those yet to come.

Alli's Story

I've told you all this so that, trusting me, you will be unshakable and assured, deeply at peace. In this godless world you will continue to experience difficulties. But take heart! I've conquered the world.
—John 16:33 (MSG)

"Daddy and I are getting married to my new mommy." That's what three-year-old Allison Jo told everyone she met. It's how she kept those who loved her on high alert over the several months of preparation for a wedding none of the adults in her life would have imagined possible a year earlier.

A photo taken at a wedding shower for her new mom and Alli Jo celebrates the childlike dreams of a little girl as she thinks about "our wedding day." At three, stuffed animals and a mommy are the surround sounds of your life. Alli couldn't wait for life to be as it should be.

Allison's first mommy (we call her Mom Stephanie) had a massive heart attack while the two of them were out to lunch with a friend. She died several days later. Alli was two years and four months old when "Mommy went to live with Jesus."

Six months earlier, our twenty-five-year-old daughter Alicia had lost the love of her life to a similar heart attack. One of her fears, looking into the future, was that she would have no children.

Two families ripped apart by untimely deaths. Two families floundering in a destruction zone of a too-young-to-die reality scene.

Two families now brought together by shared grief, an unseen Hand, and a little girl who knew she needed a mommy.

Dave (Rusticus) and Alicia obviously had a starting point for a relationship, but it takes more than that to make a marriage work. Big decisions had to be made under increased pressure from a strong-minded and determined three-year-old. Once she got to know Alicia, Alli never let up on her demands. "I want you to be my mommy" became her mission in life.

Alicia was fully as determined "not to do anything to hurt this child who's been hurt too much already." Thankfully, God was there to make a way for the three of them and for their hurting families.

Allison became the focal point of all our adult lives early on in this journey of faith. In that same photo, I see myself peering into the future, hovering over my own daughter, not wanting anything more to harm her, or this brown-eyed little beauty who very soon would become our very own first granddaughter.

The photo tells the story of lives put back together by a God who loves us, cares for us, shares our sorrows, and heals our wounds in ways we could never imagine.

Newfound joy has a way of triumphing over abandoned dreams. By His grace we were blessed to see a new family of three come together as one.

Many lives had been affected. Everyone's joy was tempered by the past, but because of one little girl, a new sense of urgency took precedence, and hope brought sunshine into our lives again.

In this precious photo, our little girl is holding a soft stuffed animal given to her by her soon-to-be Grandma Z—that would be me. Allison Jo is sitting on the lap of her soon-to-be mommy, Alicia Joy. As families and grandparents coming together, we all found the name similarities profound. We know that God often uses the little things to help us see the big picture—His picture.

We watched, as God entered into the darkest experience of human tragedy and brought hope and renewal out of despair. God used a hurting little girl to bring two people together, and what we've come to call the "Rusticii bunch" now numbers seven and includes Alli's husband Nick.

Something to Ponder

> Look at your own life experience. Where are those special places where God reached down and opened your eyes to the possibilities that life could and truly would be good again? Celebrate them, every time you remember.

Easter Blessings

Unless a grain of wheat falls into the earth and dies, it remains
just a single grain; but if it dies, it bears much fruit.
—John 12:24 (NRSV)

As we grow older, the Easter message of hope and renewal, the
news of death forever conquered, and the promise of life abundant
and eternal become ever more meaningful. Several years ago, one
of our friends from church learned that the severe pain he was
experiencing would force him to cut short his vacation in Florida
to fly home for surgery. The football-size kidney to be removed was
the largest his doctors had seen.

Life would never be the same for this family. After a long and
difficult surgery and hospital stay, he went home to try to recover
his strength, but devastating cancer raced through his body, and
within six very short weeks he was preparing to spend his first
Easter with Jesus, his dearest Friend.

This high-volume produce farmer supplied one of the largest
grocery chains and wholesalers in our area. Little did they know
when they took the first available flight home that Ken would soon
be preparing himself to leave his wife to carry on grandparenting
and his boys to carry on the family business without his quiet but
joyful presence.

Over his brief lifespan and by example, a great father had
taught his two boys and son-in-law how to be a devoted husband
and Christian father. In time, each will know how to be a hands-on
grandpa, just as he was to his very young grandchildren.

Ken would never plant or harvest another crop, but he left a
lasting legacy of Christian character building that will be the seed
for his family to use as they continue to expand the work God had
already accomplished in his life and theirs.

The family has had many confirmations that "whoever serves
Me, the Father will honor" (John 12:26, NRSV). The funeral

service was poignant and God-centered and left no doubt about whom Ken loved and served. He entered heaven joyfully to hear, "Well done, good and faithful servant!"

A noteworthy coincidence is that before Ken was buried, our church's second oldest member and prayer warrior died. Grandma Lois had asked Ken to continue planting and harvesting crops in her fields as long as she lived. By God's timing, Ken left this earth on Tuesday and Grandma Lois followed on Thursday to meet in their eternal home.

Planting seeds for life and for eternity is over for Ken and Grandma Lois. They are reaping the rewards of a heavenly harvest, but seedtime and harvest continue for all of us. We are the sowers and the harvesters for the next generations.

Something to Ponder

➤ What lessons can be drawn from this farmer's life and a Christian father's death?
➤ How do these lessons spill over into the deeper message of Easter?

Winter White ... A Child's Delight

Winter came down to our house one night
Quietly pirouetting in on silvery-toed slippers of snow, and we,
We were children once again.
—Bill Morgan Jr. (American archivist, writer 2008)

Seems like only yesterday. Grandchildren and their neighborhood friends. Rushing home from school. Flinging down their book bags—just inside the door. No thoughts for after-school snacks. A quick potty break and they're bundled up some more to keep Mom happy. They rush gleefully out the door to catapult into cavernous mounds of powdery white stuff.

They might stop to mark their territory with a whimsically personalized snow angel. Or if the big kids agree, they might build a giant snowman or cozy fort. Responding to an invite, they'll hurry back home to lace up their skates and careen around the neighbor's backyard ice rink, feet flying, arms flailing. Occasionally the lights come on at night. Oh, the fun! What summertime sport can compete?

Another day, they'll grab their super sleds and head for the hills or build cozy warm tunnels and hideaways in tightly packed snowbanks. After all the fun, if the bribe is worth the effort, they might pick up a shovel to help Mom clear the driveway before Dad comes home.

Too soon, our only grandson is old enough to run the snowblower. The world belongs to him!

I'm sad for children outside the snowbelt. They can only dream of rolling or throwing a snowball, lifting an eager tongue to savor the delicate essence of a snowflake, or sliding down a favorite hillside with screaming friends. All this, in unrestrained abandon.

What would our snow-deprived urchins give to make angel wings or build their own Frosty the Snowman?

Like grounded storm chasers, they watch the national weather reports, green with envy, as their northland cousins cut another slice of heaven, spirits soaring with the merriment of this magical season. "Next Christmas," they beg, "may we puleeeze go to visit our cousins up north? That's all we really want for Christmas!"

***

And we, the generation of snowbirds willing to sell all and fly south to beat the wintertime blues, try to forget the wonderful feeling of curling up by the fire to read a good book.

fireplace crackles
sparks of love
rich hot cocoa
in festive mugs
—Terri Guillemets, Winter Heat, 2008

The feeling is incomparable, but reality is a callous and hard-hearted master.

Something to Ponder

➤ How would you interpret this quote by Pietro Aretino: "Let us love winter, for it is the spring of genius"?
➤ What winter whimsical memory can put a smile on your face and joy in your heart today?

Hero, My Hero ...

A mentor is someone who sees more talent and ability within
you, than you see in yourself, and helps to bring it out in you.
    —Bob Proctor

The man was a giant in my schoolgirl eyes. His teaching skills—
amazing. He projected joy and love for God, and for learning, at
all levels.

As a teenager, Hero Brat played on a successful Holland
Christian High School basketball team in 1927. I'm sure young
Hero developed a good sense of his capabilities and self-worth on
this team. I can only speculate that he was very popular. He was
obviously gifted with leadership qualities and his humble attitude
would have appealed to peers and teachers alike.

In the classroom, Mr. Brat knew how to be appropriately
serious but was naturally adept at using humor and devil's advocacy
to encourage classroom participation.

Having been a teacher myself, I smile. I can see the twinkle
in his eye as he formulated his lesson plans, setting the stage for
yet another frenzied spiritual battleground of the teens in his care.

Completely at ease with students eager to combat his antiquated
views, he allowed us to boldly assert the overthrow of the senseless
traditions of our Dutch ancestors, or simply battle for the thrill of
the kill, but we were always forced to hone our mental acuity skills
to meet his ground rules: "You must have a strong defense."

He loved it when someone picked up the gauntlet flung down
at some point during his lecture. He would let us work ourselves
into a frenzy while we fought for our own prideful viewpoint.

I was never one to head for the spotlight, but in this class—
with his gentle prodding, I often picked up that gauntlet.

Before the class ended, Mr. Brat would dispel any doubt as to
what was biblical and doctrinally sound. He was the epitome of

wisdom, wit, and all things worthy. Third hour Ref Doc (Reformed Doctrine) was anything but a sleep zone for me.

He knew what we, his mentees, couldn't have known about ourselves. Our senior year would be our awakening to the world around us. For some of us, it would be an entrance to the field of lifelong learning, and I am forever grateful for his input.

As a maturing high school student I knew his world was the one I wanted for myself. I wanted to be learn-ed, like Mr. Brat. I wanted to go to college and marry someone who loved learning as much as Mr. Brat. As much as I did! But college was not an option for me as the oldest of eight. Not as far as I could see.

Midway through my senior year, one unforgettable day, Mr. Brat began walking down the hall with me on my way to class. In his easygoing style, he asked what preparations I was making for college. He noted that I had already volunteered and gone on a Summer Workshop in Missions trip (SWIM) prior to my senior year, and he saw what I didn't see for myself. I don't remember my response, but his reply startled me. He told me I needed to get ready and sign up to take the ACTS.

Dad always promised that if I would stay home and "help Mom," he would make sure I could go on to college—someday. I thought he was being nice but not very realistic. Now, someday was here, but the wherewithal was nowhere in sight.

With no one my age in the neighborhood, I had limited interests outside the family. Going back and forth on my bike to practice the organ for a Sunday evening service was a treat, not a burden. No formal lessons—just a love for music and a desire to play that beautiful instrument. Makes me shudder today, as I allow my mind to go there! Those poor souls!

Tuition fees scared me silly. I'm not a particularly persistent person, so I assumed the obvious: Mom and Dad would never be able to afford college for any of us, and being the oldest, how could I leave Mom with all the kids? My baby sister Deb was still tiny when I graduated high school!

Were there scholarships for poor country kids? How would Mom manage? I was the happy homemaker while Mom was free to do her gardening and all other necessary mom stuff. I loved cooking and baking, making a nice dinner, and taking care of babies. I also loved the mission trips that brought new perspectives to my life.

Mr. Brat promised he would help. He encouraged Mom and Dad to explore all the options. Somehow, they had always found a way, by God's grace, to provide what was necessary for their growing family...but this was very different, I knew.

I remember going to take the ACTS with a terrible stress headache—a common occurrence for me. Mom waited for me for hours, sitting in the car, in a strange Grand Rapids neighborhood, possibly pregnant and with a toddler.

That summer I left for another six weeks on a second SWIM trip to Paterson, New Jersey.

How did that work? I have no idea! I suppose I took Dad at his word. He and Mom encouraged me every step of the way. I wonder if I was perceptive enough to take God at His Word, that He would supply all my needs according to His rich storehouse of blessings (Philippians 4:19).

Years later I found an Edison quotation that spoke volumes and reminded me of Mr. Brat's gift to his students. Edison encourages us to believe in our own potential, knowing that "if we did all the things we were capable of, we would literally astound ourselves."

Mr. Brat cleared my clouded-over blue eyes so I could realize the potential he (and God) saw in me, a self-effacing, insecure teenager. Thank you, Mr. Brat! My life is everything and more than you led me to believe it could be.

Edited on November 15, 2013, on what would have been Mom's ninetieth birthday.

Something to Ponder

➤ Who in your life has encouraged you to be more and do more than your limited vision allowed?

➤ How did or how does God fit into the plan(s) you have for your life?

➤ Where is He taking you today that makes life worthwhile?

A Lifetime of Living Green

They will still produce fruit in old age.
They will be full of sap and green.
—Psalm 92:14 (WEB)

Al had spent a number of evenings prepping and spray-painting my favorite patio set of rusting rocking chairs. We were happy with the results.

Soft limey green, perfect for the side deck of the house, here on Green Lake. From there the view is restful and tree-lined as far as the eye can see, while the road winds gracefully along South Shore. I love this little deck, especially in the morning. I can watch the traffic slowly progressing up the hill and smell the morning dew on the towering pines. The birds are already arguing and jostling for a perch on the birdfeeder.

Once the kids and buses are on their way, it is peaceful and quiet. Perfect for devotions or Bible study.

Al wonders why I have such a penchant for green. He's not the rocking chair sort, but he humors me tonight.

"Green goes with everything, inside and out," I say. Rocking back and forth, I'm celebrating a rare evening—sitting with my favorite guy and a peaceful mind-set.

I tell him I'm quite sure *green* is one of God's favorite colors. He splashes it liberally throughout His creation. The color wheel He uses embraces a broad spectrum of greens—for plants and crops, for artful expression, and better yet, for growing people on the inside, especially those willing to devote time and energy to stay *fresh and green* (NIV)—heart, soul, and mind.

Going through the collection of essays loosely bound in the file, *Living Green*, I struggle to clarify for myself what they all have in common. Some date back more than seven years. All are casually written, to leave a simple legacy for family and friends.

Several years later, the leitmotif, or the challenge of retirement landed sweetly but heavily in my lap. Never one to ease back on life, I spent more time writing, and soon I felt the pulse of God urging me to write for a broader audience—one that would advance His kingdom, first of all.

I had no idea how that would change my focus, since my perspective hadn't drastically changed. I simply felt that my writing style had grown up since I first started. It seemed also to have taken on a mind of its own. It wasn't just memoir anymore. There was an inner voice propelling me to be more inclusive in my imagined audience—more than grandkids and great-grandkids and a few friends and relatives.

I had often included Scripture verses in my writing. I grew up with a Christian school education, after all—from kindergarten to a master's degree at age fifty. There should be some signs of mental and spiritual growth after all that!

Today, the stroke of a pen and the clicks on my keyboard bring meaning and purpose to my days.

***

Dad died of pancreatic cancer when he was seventy-two—my age, exactly. Dad and Mom were married fifty years. Lord willing, Al and I will celebrate fifty years this summer.

Sitting quietly, I pray, *Thank You, Lord, for this very special time in my life. I'm grateful to be here! Some of my friends and family haven't lived to enjoy their golden years. Some live with painful disabilities. Others have no idea what to do with their time. Thanks for gifting me with all-consuming desire to tell Your stories while sharing my own. Thank you for allowing me to enjoy each day, celebrating the blessings I have and the stories I've been given to share.*

Occasionally, my mind wanders far afield—back to an old pity-party workshop. "Who really cares, and why would anyone want to read what I write? Who am I to think I can write well enough to publish?" Rejection looms large for most word tinkerers.

I have to make a conscious decision—again and again, to leave this in the hands of the One who knows the number of my days and the assignment He has for me to complete. Then, I ask for His blessing on what is and will be accomplished—in His own good time.

***

During these last valuable years—may I call them the wisdom years?—I've grown steadily more certain about what *living green* demands. Seniors tell it like it is when they say, Old age is not for sissies. Well, neither is the Christian life for sissies or cowards. There's really no call (and no demand) for rocking chair saints.

In a world of muddied confusion, with traditional values being discarded as easily as yesterday's tech toys, it is important to anchor one's mind on the promises of the Word and Spirit for our eyes to be opened to growing and greening thanks-living.

Something to Ponder

- How does your own idea of *living green* match up to the ideas presented in this essay?
- What does the concept of *living green* mean to you at this stage of your life?
- Determine to show that your life is green and growing, especially in the study of God's Word.

The World of Words

Gracious Words are like a honeycomb,
sweetness to the soul and health to the body.
—Proverbs 16:24 (NRSV)

During my preschool years we lived only a short distance from my maternal grandparents in a drafty old rental farmhouse on their large farm. I was relatively free to run across a well-worn path in the field to their big old farmhouse where there was always someone to talk with or listen to my childish banter.

Grandma and Grandpa were actively raising eleven children after my mother—second of thirteen—married. That farmhouse was my favorite place to be, and I easily tucked myself in as number fourteen. My youngest aunt was only three when I was born, so loneliness was never a part of my life.

I enjoyed the constant activity of farm life and the verbal connections of a large and busy family. True, my world didn't extend much farther than the two farmhouses and church on Sunday, but there was no lack of conversation.

My youngest aunts and I talked with great excitement about the new calves. We talked to the horses and dogs and kitties that roamed the farm. We loved the soft feel of baby "peeps," which Mom raised to nine weeks. All the enticement of childhood stories was ours to enjoy in a real life setting.

Kindergarten, and my kindergarten teacher, opened another door to the world, and I loved riding the school bus with aunts and uncles. I could stay all day "like the big kids," and I loved it. I know Mom felt differently about her young five-year-old being away all day, but how hard could it be? She had two toddlers to keep her busy.

I was drawn like a magnet to reading and writing. Math? Not so much. I remember a child's dictionary in our classroom. I loved to connect the picture with the word on the page. I would laugh at the cute or funny picture and then spell the word out loud: "C-A-T, cat. D-O-G, dog." Words were amazing!

First grade, however, presented an unforeseen difficulty. I was left-handed (wrong) in a right-handed world (right). The theory was: tie the child's left hand behind her back during writing exercises and for meals—to force her to use and eventually prefer her right hand. So before supper, Mom would (unwillingly, sadly) tie my left hand to the back of the chair with a towel. During school hours my teacher would do the same before penmanship time. Many tears flowed, at school and at the supper table, and mine were not the only ones. It was especially hard because I loved to write and work with words. This only stymied my creativity.

Dad, a resolute left-hander, finally went to talk to the teacher. Or was it the principal? That ended the shackles. It has always been my belief and excuse that I have poor penmanship because of the trauma of that year. And because I've always been unhappy with my penmanship, I have a greater love for my writing buddy, the computer—greater even than my purple gel pens.

Something to Ponder

➢ What do you remember about words when you were very young?
➢ Do you have good memories about learning to use words?
➢ How do *words* serve you, now, at this stage of your life?

Too Soon

> I know that there is nothing better for them than to be happy
> and enjoy themselves as long as they live. ... It is God's gift that
> all should eat and drink and take pleasure in all their toil.
> —Ecclesiastes 3:12–13 (NRSV)

Labor Day weekend is the grand finale for summer settlers here on Green Lake—and most other lakes. Families of cottagers along South Shore are hauling in boats and docks and shore stations. Others are cleaning and carrying lawn furniture inside for winter storage. Summer planters are emptied and decks swept clean one last time.

I understand the sad little faces of kids and the hunched shoulders of teens enlisted to haul and to help. Belongings are loaded into the family van by apathetic hands and hearts, as summer friends and summer water sports are bid *adios, amigos.*

Past insight allows me to sense the tension mounting in the hearts of moms and dads. It's time to propel themselves and their offspring back into a fast-paced routine: alarm clocks, shopping for school supplies and clothes, homework, sports practice, games, and messy rooms. Add to this jobs, careers, endless carpooling and Crock-Pot or insta-pot suppers. And don't forget Wednesday night church activities—for the whole family.

Thankfully, an occasional ice- or snowstorm brings it all careening to a halt. Yeah for Michigan. Pure Michigan!

I feel a bit rebellious and whisper softly, while I'd really like to scream, "It's too early! Don't let it end so soon! September sun is golden, and we have all this to ourselves! October color and burning leaves mean bonfires and more s'mores. Don't go yet!"

They look at me with envy, sitting nonchalant in my comfy lounge. Oh, well! I smile. Thank You, God, for another day to be thankful ... for yet another day! We who are blessed to live here year-round know the best of autumn is still to come.

Reality being what it is, we're all eager to get on with it. Life is for living, and we will play and work and serve and give, and in our hearts we will hold the promise of another season of peaceful days and summer sun.

***

It's early morning, and I'm sitting on the second floor side deck facing east. As the sun peeks through the pines, I look on the neighborhood scene below. Adults scurry about, work mode ready. Jostling kids with weighted book-bags—some eager and some resistant toward the day taking shape. A bus stops. Red lights blink. An impatient motorcyclist idles noisily behind. Birds squawk. Some sing. Motors rumble, and vehicles back into the roadway. All the while, a woodpecker rattles in the rafters of an abandoned garage just across the way.

It's my Green Lake wake-up call.

Down the hill, the magnificent maples are inspired. Leaves are turning shades of auburn and ginger gold. A wide expanse of color covers the pavement below. I savor the earthy smell. The vibrant greens of summer are losing the battle of the seasons, but I remind myself that *autumn is truly my favorite time of year.*

Construction workers fire up their electric drills and hammers. The day is begun. Too soon.

Something to Ponder

> ➤ Consider: What is good about the changing of seasons?
> ➤ How about the changing of your life seasons?
> ➤ What would be an important step to take toward preparing for the next season of your life?

Like an Eagle

> You yourselves have seen ... how I carried you on
> eagles' wings and brought you to myself. Now if you
> obey me fully and keep my covenant, then out of all
> nations you will be my treasured possession.
> —Exodus 19:4–5 (NIV)

Living on the Gerald R. Ford flight path, with a picture window to the sky, we were blessed to watch the late-night show of outbound flights—from the comfort of a bed faced in the right direction.

We had decided, wisely or foolishly, to live without drapes or blinds in our third-floor master bedroom, not wanting to hinder our view of water, trees, and sky. We never regretted the decision, even though it was primarily based on the cost of window covering for yet another wall of windows.

I, who chose not to do as my dear husband often suggests, "Just close your eyes!" had many opportunities to watch as planes angle off in various directions—on schedule, nearly every night. I knew the times and flight patterns each would take.

I loved watching these phantoms of light glide slowly up into the night sky and then over the house and out of sight. Many silent prayers sent them on their way.

The distant roar only reached us as the plane passed overhead, but the constancy of these silver birds was always reassuring.

I recalled those very dark days following 9/11/01. The new millennium was still in its infancy, and memory had not erased our concerns leading up to the New Millennial celebration of 2000. We came to know it as the Y2K (Year Two Thousand) experience.

I remembered the panic some of my high school students experienced prior to Christmas Break of 1999. We had been warned for months to expect computer system failures, possible plane crashes, and extended power outages—all at the stroke of midnight, New Year's Eve.

Happy 2000!

I had lots of opportunity to exercise my own faith in earnest discussions with students who overflowed into my office, nearly unhinged, after hearing a new concern in the news, in their classes, or on the grapevine.

I was privileged to encourage students to pray, really pray, for His direction and guiding hand. We were Christian schoolteachers, so we could pray for God to direct the scientists and computer wizards—many of them working frantically to tame or turn aside this potentially unruly beast.

Teachers shared their faith and reminded students that God truly was in control. He would see us through to the New Year, no matter the what-ifs. And so we prayed, sometimes together.

I confess, it was not the usual, but we were sincere.

On New Year's Day, we all breathed a giant sigh of relief and promptly forgot all about those fear-filled days.

Was it smart science that prevented our demise? Or had our prayers been answered in a truly big way?

Today, my grandkids ask, "What's Y2K?" while I stutter over *LGBTQ … What?*

Twenty-one months after Y2K, the night sky turned black and silent. No air traffic flowed in any direction for several days after the horrendous attacks of 9/11. And then only under heavy restrictions.

A gut-wrenching shared grief and loss enveloped the entire country as we mourned the catastrophic loss of nearly three thousand lives. Business associates and employers from around the world, working in the World Trade Center and the Pentagon, along with the fated Flight 93 passengers and crew who died in a Pennsylvania field on this infamous day, were ripped from their families, and friends were torn from friends.

Without faith, it was a time nearly devoid of hope. Christians and nonbelievers alike struggled. We feared for our country, our way of life, our freedoms. A fragile and tenuous future hung heavy over the entire free world.

Why? How did this happen? These were questions no one seemed able to answer.

After settling down to a new reality we realized once again the faithfulness of an amazing God. Though many lives had been lost and many more people's lives would never be the same, He had brought the country through a great tragedy and would carry us into the future, whatever it held.

A shiver runs through me as I think of what our grandkids and their parents worry about today—the opioid epidemic, school shootings and bombings, suicides and sex changes, child molestations and sex trafficking ….

Anything new to us is nothing new to God. He often uses painful circumstances to draw us back and into a closer relationship with Him by inviting us to shelter under His all-powerful wings, knowing this is where we will again find joy for living.

***

As I edit this piece, written some years ago, I must add a postscript.

A short few weeks ago, America experienced another heart-rending blow to our security—personal and national. The Las Vegas Massacre (10/1/17), where nearly sixty people died and five-hundred or more were injured, occurred only days after Hurricane Maria (9/17/17) devastated most of Puerto Rico and other popular tourist islands. All of this followed on the heels of Hurricane Harvey, which was accompanied by ravaging floods in Houston, Florida, Louisiana, and elsewhere. Pain and horrific loss seems unrestrained.

All during this time, wildfires raced through a wide swath of beautiful country in California, shocking the nation once again with massive destruction, loss of life and property.

Then, several days ago, more than two dozen parishioners, from eighteen months to seventy-seven years of age, were gunned down.

Many more were critically injured at the hands of a deranged killer. Horror unimaginable, during a Sunday morning worship service in a small church, in a small town, and once again, in Texas.

By the time you read this, other atrocities will undoubtedly have occurred. Does anyone outside the Christian faith have answers for the calamities in nature and the corruption we see in society and the world around? Who, besides God, can provide sanctuary?

Francis Schaeffer's book *How Should We Then Live?*, written more than forty years ago (1976), grapples with the issues of Christians living in a sin-sick, volatile, and deteriorating world. In this reality, secularism leads a vicious attack and clambers gleefully into the seat we Protestants proudly and rather smugly held since the founding days of America.

Prior to the writing of Schaeffer's book, the Supreme Court enacted the Roe v. Wade abortion on demand decision (1973). Men like Schaeffer and other Christian leaders were sounding the alarm, but the outcry of most believers was sadly missing.

The time from the 1963 Supreme Court decision to reject God, His Word, and prayer in our public schools to the abortion on demand decision of 1973 was a brief ten years.

Followers of Christ now live in a vastly different world, possibly because our generation didn't heed the voice of prophetic giants when it would have been easier to turn a leaking ship toward harbor.

Today, Christians open their sleepy eyes to a world where Christianity, its moral code, and biblical principles have been sidelined and subdued. In the vacuum created by our new social justice laws, standard bearers—you and I and our Christian leaders—must fight doubly hard to win back the heritage that is rightly ours through the God-given foresight of our nation's Founders.

We no longer live on a flight path, but I welcome each flight as a reminder that life goes on at His command. God reigns, and all—yes, all is well. No matter the circumstances or devastations of life, God has not lost control of His world, His children, or their lives. He says to us, "Do not let your hearts be troubled. Believe in God, believe [trust] also in Me. In My Father's house there are many dwelling places …. I go to prepare a place for you …. I will come again and take you to myself" (John 14:1–3 ESV).

Something to Ponder

➤ Knowing that our earthly life is uncertain, where are you investing your time and energy here on earth?

➤ God's hand of blessing promises a beautiful homecoming. The journey, no doubt, will be precarious at times. We might come sliding in, out of breath, or hobbling in with bruises and scars, but once we're there, an amazing forever life begins, better than anything imaginable. We will truly have found the perfect place to live and to enjoy Him for eternity. Do you really believe it? Then go and tell!

➤ Who do you know who might need a word of encouragement to help them along in their own journey toward the Light?

Technology on the Loose

The difference between technology and slavery
is that slaves are fully aware that they are not free.
—Nassim Nicholas Taleb

We of the baby boomer generation are compelled to stumble along yet another learning curve as the world streaks by, chasing the next and newest specter of technology.

Every facet of our harried society threatens to shut us out if we allow ourselves to become technologically incompetent by refusing to keep up with the latest tech trends.

Recently, we shared brunch at Community Restaurant in Zeeland, MI, to celebrate Aunt Ali's ninety-eighth birthday. We gave her many nice options, but she chose the old familiar down-home restaurant, where the staff welcomed her with open arms and were ready to share in the festive occasion. She knew they would settle her in a safe corner with her walker, her nieces, and her kids (all of us over fifty-five).

From a mental standpoint, she has amazing ability to remember events from the past and conversations that happened months and years ago. She has a contagious interest in everything going on around her.

Of course, we teased her for ordering her piece of pie as she passed the lighted case—before she sat down. She laughed, knowing we were thinking of the joke about seniors eating dessert first—just in case they didn't make it to the next course.

"You don't want to take any chances," she said. So most of us ordered pie—in her honor, of course.

She saw someone on a cell phone and needed to tell us about how her kids had tutored her and tutored some more on how to use "that crazy phone"—her oldest is seventy-six years young. "It was horrible!" Then, eyes sparkling, she laughed her naughty little laugh. "It took a long time and a lot of talking, but I won the battle. Oh, I'm so happy with my old table phone. *It works just fine!*"

This was a perfect launch pad to our next topic: kids and their tech toys.

Our needs and wants are not the same as those of the younger generation, but most of us are mentally competitive enough to do what it takes to stay in the game—whatever that means to us. We worry that we are losing our kids, our grandkids, and our friends, having been robbed of eye contact with them. They pretend to listen, while fingers scroll and eyes scan.

We console ourselves. They say we've come from a wiser generation—yeah for me, one of the earliest baby boomers! But look around. We can be drawn into the same deceptive web as our offspring. We love those games on our phones, iPods, laptops; keeps the brain cells active, we think. For some of us, these games relieve us from boredom or the frustration we feel as we think about the disturbed and troubled world around us.

The flood of gadgetry has come to dominate our American culture. An obscene amount of our income (or retirement funds) can be spent on these personal tech items—all needing continual updates and upgrades.

Drones and driverless cars and buses are popping up everywhere. Extreme, yes, but not for long.

A quick scan of how much money and time was spent on updates and tech equipment over the past year would be enlightening. If you have kids, you might want to do this together. You'll be amazed at your spending habits.

More and more apps, many of them free, appear to have a single goal—to draw the user deeper into a self-centered world of disconnect while promising the opposite. We see its damaging effects on schoolwork, home life, and the ability to communicate verbally with friends and family.

I have no doubt Aunt Ali would agree with Albert Einstein, Nobel Prize winner in physics (1879–1955). He made this sad prediction: "I believe that the abominable deterioration of ethical standards stems primarily from the mechanization and depersonalization of our lives, a disastrous byproduct of science and technology." Written possibly during my own growing-up years, it sends shock waves through me as I write today.

Some would argue, and I agree, never has there been more fingertip information available, but these same tools, created to advance our productivity and enjoyment of life, have the unprecedented capacity to accelerate our moral and spiritual demise.

Social media in all their forms have, at the very least, the potential to steal precious time from children who deserve personal time and space with Mom and Dad—cozied up in a reading corner, with real books, able to carry them far out and away, into a wide and beautiful world of growing and learning. Or to enhance family dinner conversations and dialogue.

Not to be taken lightly, all these (internet, TV, or—fill in the blank) are wonderful add-ons to our lives, but too quickly they become dangerous marauders of time and our physical and spiritual well-being. polluted programming and hedonistic entertainment all prey heavily on our young people and our children.

How then, should Christians live in this detoured but technologically elite society? How can we safeguard our families? In Job 1:10 Satan recognizes the hedge or the fence God has placed around Job and admits he cannot penetrate it without God's permission. Wow! Let's hold tight to this thought and promise!

Our recourse, then, is to pray continually for God to put a hedge around each one of us and our loved ones—wherever we and they may be in our walk of faith, or in our rebellion—just as David recognized God's protection, even from himself, when he said, "You hem me in, behind and before, and lay your hand upon me" (Psalm 139:5 NRSV). The hedge, the safety net God provides, is really the sword of His Spirit, which is the Word.

Technology's *gifts* have become the devil's primary weapons for breaking down the walls or defenses of our twenty-first-century social order.

We are duty bound to live with a broad awareness of the dangers of whatever devices we allow ourselves and our children to use, and when we pray, we must do so in humility, knowing God can bless our efforts and secure the hedge, or He can choose to let us suffer the consequences of our neglect or disobedience. If we are the adults, *vigilance* is our appropriate response.

Think of all the resources you and I are fortunate to have and how we are meant to live, as blessed people who spend more time meeting the needs of a hurting world than swaddling our own self-interests.

Lord, we know the battle belongs only and always to You. We are humbled to know that we are powerless outside the hedge You have placed around us. Keep us strong, clear-minded, and vigilant about the thieves and robbers in our lives and homes.

Something to Ponder

➢ I encourage you to complete the survey suggested toward the beginning of this essay. Count the cost outlay, and estimate the amount of (non-business) time spent with your devices every day.

➢ Add up the family's estimates, and put that number down for all to see. Then answer your own questions about your family's personal use of time and technology.

➢ Where does Jesus, in His Spirit, live and move today? Is He is alive in our hearts and at the center as He deserves, or is a thorough cleaning process called for?

A Lost Chord, a Dream, and a Song

> He put a new song in my mouth,
> a song of praise to our God.
> —Psalm 40:3 (NRSV)

An accomplished musician and writer, my sister Shar has performed for appreciative audiences in many different venues, large and small, for many years. One of her CDs highlights a poignant song titled "Audience of One."

The words, the music, and her magnificent voice all captured my thoughts and heart at first hearing. Did she really write the text and the melody and then pull it all together with this mesmerizing accompaniment?

The answer was yes, yes, and yes.

Our songbird Dad taught us by example to allow the music to come alive in our hearts and to personalize every phrase and musical line. Shar's large and scattered family are inspired by her efforts to share the message of the hymns and songs of our past around the world.

Late one night, after a half-hearted decision to begin the journey of producing a second book, I was startled from sleep after a vivid dream. It came as another moment of truth for this questioning sojourner:

I was seated at the keyboard onstage, in a large auditorium. Completely alone. As in childhood, I just started playing a simple, improvised melody, adding harmony and chords as I meandered along.

Gradually, elusive and shadowy sounds turned bolder and more dramatic, moving then like an effervescent stream, picking up tempo and complexity. Chords evolved with strident and aggressive resonance, then dissolved in joyful resolution, invigorating my spirit more than any music I had ever aspired to write or perform.

Beautiful strains and sounds spilled out and over the keyboard, storming out of a place inside I did not know—as though inspired for a royal audience.

Then a rare and sweet sound rose, strangely peaceful, beautifully tranquil. In brighter harmonic tones than I knew to exist—the accomplishment of a lifetime.

As the music soared toward a finale, I became aware of a crowd of people clapping and cheering. I finished and found myself clapping along with the audience, exhilarated and completely humbled by the exquisite music we had heard.

A lone figure appeared on the bench beside me. Together, we had witnessed something magnificent. He murmured, "You wrote this? You memorized it?"

I confessed, "Neither."

I woke but didn't stir. Couldn't move. I lay, wondering if and how this connected to my future. *Could it be just another dream?*

The answer came quickly. I had been here before. I recognized again God's call to action. I got up to sit quietly in my office, unable to fully comprehend the gift of insight I had just been given.

Still fearful of the unknown, I listened again to Shar's music. This sister has spent many solitary but precious midnight hours at her own beloved piano keyboard. Giving back and receiving from her Audience of One:

The concert is over, the people are gone.
Applause now has ended.
The room is still. Where is my audience, when I return to reality?
… Who am I striving to please night
and day? Where are they now?
… In the darkest of nights when I cannot sing?
Who is my audience when I'm questioning?
Jesus cares. He knows. He answers my prayers.
… I'll live my best for Him! My Audience of One.
(Words and Music by Shar Boerema, 2000)

Having listened over and over to the soulful words and music, they have become my own. Christian ministry is servanthood—giving to others on a sacrificial level. A task conceivable only with an outside but incoming source—my *Audience of One.*

***

The immortalized words of "The Lost Chord" come from a poem written by Adelaide Anne Procter in 1858. The words, the poetry, begged to be set to music but it was nearly twenty years before the great English composer Sir Arthur Sullivan finally accomplished the task in 1877. As many writers and composers can confirm, coalescing the vibrancy of the words or poetry with the perfect composition often demands a long and arduous struggle.

Ten years later, in1888, Thomas Edison introduced his Perfected Phonograph to a cultured London audience. For the first music ever to be recorded, he chose "The Lost Chord."

I grew up with a deep affection for this stunning rendition of poetry set to music. Whenever I sat down to "work over" or compose a simple piece of music, I would search for that ear-splitting moment when all comes together as one resounding YES!

Stunning thought: When we arrive at heaven's portals, we will begin to experience the magnificent and superlative *harmony of the spheres.* With one heart and mind, all will hear it—in one perfect and newly preferred genre.

Greek philosopher, Pathagoras identified this "harmony of the spheres" in early 6th Century BC. Sadly, this great thinker did not recognize God as Creator of the spheres.

Pastor Maltie Babcock's hymn of praise, in 1901, expressed the thoughts of the Christian's heart when he wrote these words, *This is My Father's World.* *...All nature sings and round me rings the music of the spheres.* He died young (age 43) before the words were set to the delightful tune of an old English hymn, *Terra Beata*

(*Beautiful World*). We sang it often in our classrooms, especially in springtime, with a teacher or student banging out the tune and a touch of melody on the old upright (if there was one).

As I remember, the available pianos went to the rooms where there was a teacher or student pianist. Lucky for my classroom!

As I contemplated last night's dream, these familiar lines drifted through my mind—words and music I knew at a heart level:

… my fingers wandered idly, over the noisy keys.
I knew not what I was playing, or what I was dreaming then,
But I struck one chord of music like the
sound of the great Amen!
It may be that only in Heav'n I shall hear that Grand Amen!

Someday, I smiled, there will be a Grand Amen. A pure, sweet, and perfect trumpet call will signal the entrance of the bride of Christ into the kingdom prepared for His chosen. No one will miss it.

So here I am, in front of another keyboard—and my computer screen. Here lies the body of essays holding many years of musings hidden deep in the archives. Waiting to be given a voice.

Something to Ponder

➤ Have you ever had a dream so real, you knew it was meant to be a guidepost for your future?
➤ Do you have a dream that you haven't yet brought to light?
➤ Have you set realistic goals, and are you working to advance the deep thoughts of your heart into reality? The right time to begin? Now!

Just Breathe

With joy you will draw water from the wells of salvation.
And you will say …
Give thanks to the Lord,
call on His name …
—Isaiah 12:3–4 (NRSV)

We had lived on Green Lake for about fifteen years when *change*, ominous but familiar, hammered at my door. It was the summer of 2011, but I felt as if the icy winds of winter had pursued me right into the midst of a heat wave. I felt cornered, lost, and without direction.

I prayed for renewal and a new purpose for living. Days, weeks, and months went by before the answer came, quiet but strong and firm. I recognized His voice. God was about to shake up my world once again.

This time I was waiting but not yet willing. What I heard didn't make sense, in light of my weak-kneed prayers, but here it was: *Trust Me. Stop looking for a new position. You are exactly where I want you to be. So breathe! Just breathe. I will direct your path, all the way into the future. It's time to make writing a priority. I want you to write for Me. For My Glory.*

I heard, but I had no response. I asked for peace and a compass in the midst of my own mental maelstrom.

Soon after, we were traveling by coach, through mile after mile of green hillsides, sweeping highlands, and the serene valleys of Ireland. I couldn't help but unwind—journaling as always, wherever we travel.

So peaceful and picturesque, these hills and highlands. Sheep grazing contentedly. An ancient country's people moving about, clearly unfrenzied, outwardly at peace with nature and themselves.

Tiny pastel homes dot the countryside. Their residents, happy and content (I believed) with minimal creature comforts. So unlike Americans who hurry and scurry about, futility swallowing our efforts to make every move and minute count. Feeling driven to do more, earn more, so we can have more. Always more. To add to the hodgepodge of stuff and home-turf collections.

***

Quiet times of contemplation, though we seldom seek them, are exactly what we need and what God intends. He wants us to stop. Long enough to breathe—just breathe.

And then He invites us to drink from the well He provides. It will bring new life. Restore life.

The water is crystal clear. Inviting. But the well, you can see, is infinitely deep. Its depth even fearsome. He assures us the water will be as refreshing as the pure air we are now breathing. There will be no limits.

We remember the words of Revelation: "Never again will they thirst … for the Lamb … will lead them to springs of living water" (Revelation 7:16–17, NIV).

***

The freedom of having feet dangle in pendulum motion, with no attachment to the ground, can hardly be *wordified*. The porch swing I love had awaited my return. The cacophony of flowering blooms along my garden wall tempt and draw the butterflies, hummingbirds, and honeybees. It's a merry feast for the eyes when these creature delights settle on waiting buds and flowers.

Waves lap quietly at the shoreline, and I listen to the melodic offerings of early morning songsters. I'm inspired with the inexhaustible variety of cloud formations over the water and stunned once again as an artist of infinite design skills begins to color the sky with broad strokes. His palette, clean and fresh, communicates the indescribable grandeur of His world. His hand shapes it all together in a morning anthem of praise.

Late in the day, after a full day of writing accomplishments, I face a setting sun. I take a moment to relish the happy sounds of children and families playing on the beach or flying by on a giant tube, screaming and laughing, holding on for dear life.

Too soon, it is sundown. The hum of pontoons on evening parade brings another precious day to conclusion. Too soon, I find myself mesmerized by the glimmer of a setting sun slowly being swallowed up by the horizon.

Amy Grant recently repopularized one of my favorite childhood songs, written more than a hundred years ago. Simply and with clarity, Amy sings the old song for the next generation:

> This is my Father's world,
> And to my listening ears,
> All nature sings, and round me rings
> The music of the spheres.
> —Maltbie D. Babcock, 1901

Something to Ponder

➤ Can you look back on a time of bewilderment about the future, when God took you aside and brought you to the place where you could find peace and security?

➤ Where is that special place you can go to savor a few minutes of simply breathing in the goodness of life?

➤ Have you found a way to share the lessons you learned in the *wasteland*? Or the joys you have found in the center of His will?

Save or Delete?

He [the Sovereign Lord] has sent me to bind up the brokenhearted,
to proclaim freedom for the captives
and release from darkness for the prisoners …
To comfort all who mourn …
to bestow on them **a crown of beauty**
instead of ashes,
the oil of joy
instead of mourning,
and **a garment of praise**
instead of a spirit of despair.
—Isaiah 61:1–3 (NIV)

Before I began the actual process of publishing *She Walks in Beauty and Endless Light*, my blood pressure would skyrocket toward an all-out panic attack whenever the thought came to mind.

Gently, little by little, with God's help, I abandoned my security blankets. No more excuses. The *Who* calling my name is the One who had commissioned me earlier to *write these things down and tell what you have learned*—living life *between the dots*.

I've learned how to step away from some of my greater fears and simply *let it go*. This time I know more about the process, but there is still a good bit of tension about what essays (I have many) are worthy of publishing. Mental due dates have come and gone, several times actually.

My first writing coach had encouraged our little group of wannabes and struggling writers to compose an essay before the next class about "the thing that draws you like a magnet". Or, if we were up for a real challenge, "the one experience you never expected to be able to share … with anyone. Once you have finished, you are free to hit *Save* or *Delete*." Her lesson for us was to write without boundaries and then save only what we, as writers, deemed worthy of an edit.

I chose—did you doubt it?—to take the challenge. Conquer the one thing that kept rising to the surface in my life, causing pain, anger, and at times discouragement. I had forgiven the guilty party, but the actual experience still owned a part of me.

Finally, after another wrestling match with the devil and a covering of prayer, I was able to find a way to turn a dreadful memory into a compelling story that God has, on occasion, asked me to share.

After spending a good amount of tears and time, writing it all down, editing, revising, and editing again, a peaceful acceptance and readiness settled over me. I realized a sense of eagerness to begin the work I was called to do. It was freeing to know that I could always hit *Save* or *Delete* on anything I produced—on my own computer, that is! This time, I hit *Save*.

With this new perspective, I tell my stories with the added dimension of God's love and forgiveness. It is amazing to me how that brightens the story line. Going forward, I find, nothing satisfies more than to hit Save, however late or early the hour, knowing that one more paragraph or one more essay is polished and ready to bless someone somewhere.

Something to Ponder

➢ Have you experienced the truth of God taking something awful or unusable from your past and seen Him convert the rubble into something valuable in your own or someone else's life?

➢ What are the lessons you learned at His feet during that dark time? Is there someone who could benefit if you share your stories?

Seasons Come and Seasons Go

> He changes times and seasons ...
> He gives wisdom to the wise
> and knowledge to those who have understanding.
> —Daniel 2:21 (NRSV)

Seasons are more distinct here in Michigan than in many other places. When you know the difference between summer and winter in the Midwest, you also know what you have to celebrate when spring and then summer finally arrive. Nothing compares to the freedoms of summer, especially if you are young at heart and fully alive to the fun of beach-going, boating, fishing, swimming, canoeing, or whatever brings you outdoors.

These three to four months of summer are precious and priceless. All too soon, the buses roll, the book bags line the hallways, and a new season is underway.

Autumn's cooler days begin with a kaleidoscope of color in ripening fruits and veggies and the layering of comfy, cozy sweaters and cover-ups, all to signal the grand finale of summer. Once the trees take on their glorious autumn foliage, we feel the urge to get ready for the full expressions of wintertime in all its glistening splendor and darkling drabness. But even a blustery day has its bright spots—if we are wise enough to look for them.

The sun shining through the gloom of a chilly and wind-biting day can prompt the troubled soul to lift her gaze upward—if only to soak up what vitamin C might come along to raise and brighten the spirits.

We Michiganders often say, "Fall is my favorite time of year." *Really?* you might think ... incredulous! *Not summer?*

Who knows why? It's just a feeling that overtakes you.

If you use your imagination, you might feel some of the excitement of a dress rehearsal—let's say, of a wedding. There will be highs, and there will be lows, as with most dress rehearsals.

This one, however, lasts for an extended time. Every ornamental bush, shrub, and tree is getting dressed to the nines. *Pure Michigan,* we say!

Fall color tours with friends, family, or spouse can be an exhilarating feast of sights and smells. I remember the song from childhood: "Pumpkins mellow, apples yellow, tell the time of year. Nuts are falling, nature's calling. Autumn time is here" (by Ida F. Leyda).

Some of us are savoring the lingering natural beauty of the walking trails, hoping to stave off going back to the treadmill, fitness center, or mall. We know of friends who are getting into the routine of babysitting grandchildren who would otherwise be in day care. They will enjoy walks with strollers or celebrate the exuberance of a two- or three-year-old falling or jumping into a pile of rustling leaves.

Thank God for willing and able grandparents! The blessings, too numerous to count, will linger for a lifetime for both the child and grandparent.

Days ago, it was our privilege to walk with good friends along a still warm but extremely windy Grand Haven beach. With all our senses vibrating, we were well aware of the transformation in progress.

We remembered seeing last year's waves thrashing high against the pier and rocky ledges. The current weather reports threaten snow and bone-chilling winds—thrilling to see, but only from the warmth of your vehicle. It's all coming soon to a beach near us!

In Michigan, winter preparation is absolutely necessary if we want to enjoy what is soon to come marching in on every side. Urns and pots must be emptied, perennials cut back, annuals discarded, and lawn furniture stored. Winter clothing must be purchased or passed along to the next in line. And don't forget, boots! We ladies love our boots––but only if they're sexy, cuddly, or cute.

We aim to make life warm and cozy—inside, looking out. We

prepare to light the fire and gaze out the windows at our winter wonderland. Whatever it takes to feel impervious to the weather. Snow shovels and blowers set ready and waiting.

***

Although the seasons of life usually follow a predictable pattern, like the weather, we might move from summer's glow to winter's blast in the blink of an eye. Still, we can be sure that God's *planner* (for each of us) is perfectly ordered and aligned, no cross-outs, no erasing. We can trust His hand and His heart for the seasons of life that are unordered and out of sync or even life-changing.

We know that hard times will come. And they will go. Good times will return, but all at His command and in His plan.

Christine Caine, in *365 Readings and Reflections, Living Life Undaunted*, reminds us that much of our walk of faith " has to do with learning to trust the goodness and faithfulness of God despite what happens to us or … around us".

Something to Ponder

➢ Seasons of life are similar to the seasons in creation. Sometimes, though, they move in uncharted ways. What season of life do you find yourself in right now?
➢ Take time to ponder the questions that are real to you. Talk to God, and then write out your thoughts, whether or not you have answers to the questions that bubble to the surface.

Simple but Not Easy

> Simple can be harder than complex. You have to work hard
> to get your thinking clean, to make it simple. But it's worth
> it …. Once you get there, you can move mountains.
> —Steve Jobs, co-founder, Apple Computers

Spending so much time writing and editing what I hope will someday be a worthy memoir, I fully relate to the assessment of Steve Jobs. Story ideas come easily for me. I have a thick pile of scribbles and sticky notes silently gathering dust in an overflowing wicker basket under my desk.

Once I feel the urge to cover the nakedness of a story skeleton on my computer screen, it takes a few minutes to decide on a catchy title for a new essay—which may or not hold. Then I hit Save As and start writing "the bones of the story"—the way my high school English teacher suggested.

I'll pull the essay together, then I usually walk away—for a day, a week, sometimes much longer. By the time I circle back around, it seems my brain has subconsciously done some legwork of its own, and other supporting ideas rise to the surface, along with some fitting literary lines or Bible quotes. If not, in the new tradition of writers all, I'll search the Web. Pump in an idea or two, and voilà! The perfect cover line or scriptural reference to accent a newly written anecdote.

Once the piece is sketched out, I'll revisit again and again, each time to read from a new perspective—being particularly conscious of new readers and younger readers.

Anyone can tell a story, but what will it take for someone to read to the bottom of the first page, the first chapter, and all the way to the end? Does the story line draw and pull the reader on from one crisp and clear idea to the next?

If not, then it's time to take out that literary fine-tooth comb to untangle any scrambled ideas, pick at the knots begging for a little research, and figure out what is blocking a smooth finish. At first glance, it seems like a lot of work, but in the end, a satisfying story is its own reward.

Something to Ponder

> How or when in your life have you experienced the truth of Steve Jobs's words, "Simple can be harder than complex. You have to work hard to get your thinking clean to make it simple"?
> In what way does this phrase resonate with you: "Once you get there, you can move mountains"?

Reflections on a Marriage ...

> Place me like a seal over your heart,
> like a seal on your arm.
> —Song of Solomon 8:6 (NIV)

The Zs will soon be leaving beautiful Green Lake. It has been twenty-five summers and nearly twenty years since we changed our address. "No more building projects," I flatly stated. Al was somewhat earthier with his, "Feet first next time!" We were exhausted but filled with amazement at the completion of an undertaking neither of us could have fully understood at the outset.

But time moves on with breathtaking speed. Solomon's poignant reflections on time (Ecclesiastes 3:1–13 NIV) are often quoted: "There is … a time to be born and a time to die, a time to plant and a time to uproot … a time to tear down and a time to build." Looking introspectively, we might see that God instills His wisdom into our lives for us to grow in grace and to pass it along to others en route to our eternal home.

This past week I spent time going through a box, embossed with an artfully designed spray of roses. I had saved it for many years and it held long-forgotten photos, journals, and letters. I found a note I had written for Valentine's Day more than twenty years ago. It predated some heavy losses in our family circle––now complete with seven grandchildren and a granddaughter's beau.

I am grateful and humbled to say that my perspective on marriage hasn't changed much, but I value our marriage now more than ever!

Those many years ago we drove, both of us tense and quiet, to pick up wedding rings created solely for us by a designer in Kalamazoo. Did we do the right thing? Were we crazy? Mr. Engstrom promised to take the rings back if we didn't approve. But then what? *Start over?*

We were stunned and nearly speechless to see the fruits of

that lengthy personality interview conducted a month earlier, as we sat in his studio.

We've taken many risks since then, but God has been faithful during times of elation and times when we stepped out into the unknown to take one more leap of faith.

My perspective today, as I anticipate the formidable move ahead of us, downsizing more than forty-five years of living full out, is overwhelming. Fond memories and blessings too numerous to count. Some weighted with the reality of imperfections and limitations—of time, of will—or lack of persistence.

We have lived our lives investing—in children, family, friends, missions, church, career, students, and, yes, retirement.

Today we consider our investments differently. As it regards possessions, we must reverse our thinking as we choose to divest … of things superficial or having no lasting value.

John Weirick, Huffington Post's writer on faith, culture, relationships, and personal growth, notes: "Our eternal perspective affects our earthly priorities." Easy to say; not always easy to correct.

Scripture, of course, gives us more specifics about where to store up our real treasures. Here's a hint from a guy who started out as a tax collector: It is not in opening a planned retirement fund. Matthew passes along this sage advice: "Store up for yourselves treasures in heaven [because] where your treasure is, there your heart will be also" (Matthew 6:20–21 NRSV).

Something to Ponder

> Wherever you are on your journey of faith, reflect on your ideas of what makes a marriage worthwhile, doable, and even a blessing—not only to yourself, but to others?
> What are your thoughts on retirement and investments? What do you think of when you think of divesting?

Time to Get Over Ourselves

> They shall still bear fruit in old age;
> They shall be fresh and flourishing.
> —Psalm 92:14 (NKJV)

My firstborn daughter suddenly woke up to the fact that I was having another birthday. As if head-slammed with a brick, she yelled, "You are *not* turning *seventy* yet, are you, *Motherrr?*" Long, loud sigh. There it was, the crime I couldn't resist.

I took the blow and then shook it off, realizing, *She is only reckoning with her own mortality—from a daughter's perspective.* As she shuddered, facing the rolling away of years, I know she and I face the same thief of time.

And then we laughed! We knew people—loved ones and friends who weren't privileged to reach threescore and counting.

We also know that age often comes with limitations. Painful reminders that life as we've known it is gone. While youthful beauty is difficult to hold on to, with God at work in us, an inner beauty blooms and grows as we spend more time strengthening our core self by doing what He has called us to do—overcome and conquer the world in His name (see Romans 8:37). Age doesn't matter much.

Passing beauty, strength, or worldly relevance must never deflect us from our mission to be a light in a dark place. Note how quickly suicide has become a way of escape for young and old, from chronic illness, grief, betrayal, anger, depression—the list goes on. The world is desperate to hear the gospel of hope and peace, and hope thrives where true wisdom, which is "first pure, then peaceable [and] gentle," is brought to light (James 3:17 ESV).

Paul gives it to us straight: "By this time"—after all the training you have had in His Word—"you ought to be teachers" (Hebrews 5:12 ESV). So no more excuses. We are the chosen. Chosen by God to show others the way to the Truth. It's time to get over ourselves and get on with being the light we were meant to be in this very dark world.

Lord, help me live with gratitude for each day You give, to do the work You intend for me.

Something to Ponder

> What are your thoughts about aging? Are these thoughts in line with what God thinks about age and time?
> What is our mission in life if we belong to a God who has been unfailing in His faithfulness to us?

Those Golden Years

You are never too old to set another goal or dream a new dream.
—C. S. Lewis

Mom had lived her life to serve. It was her core self and the only life that resonated. When she sold the farm and moved to Royal Park Condos, she found numerous ways to serve in her new neighborhood. She would offer to do a resident's laundry and return it fresh and folded, maybe even ironed. When someone didn't show up for lunch, she would stop by to do what she could or find someone to get it done.

Late in the fall, when geraniums needed to be dumped or taken inside, Mom took it upon herself to organize and maintain a beautiful indoor greenhouse—with whatever her friends' families brought to the solarium.

She never tired of having something to do, and she loved flowers, particularly geraniums—she never met a geranium she didn't love. We were proud to see how her efforts brightened her day and that of the walkers, visitors, and staff.

Mom's gait had always been closer to that of a garden bunny being chased by a toddler. She was easily frustrated by the lollygagging turtles so many around her seemed to imitate. "It's no wonder they can't get around anymore—they don't exercise!"

But time is not always supportive of one's natural bent. She was slowing down, and we all saw the signs. She never did settle easily into her rocking chair, however.

It would have been a rare day that she didn't skip-walk down the hallway with a full bucket of water and a dustpan to clean up after herself. She would water and deadhead geraniums of all sizes, colors, and varieties and then fill the empty bucket with the remains. She must have fertilized them occasionally, because the blooms were always full and healthy.

She loved natural beauty and living a meaningful life, and

the appreciation of residents and visitors was all the reward she needed. It got her up in the morning and kept her going through the sometimes dreary days of a Michigan cellar winter.

***

"Gramma Great" was headed over to see the twins—Alicia's and Dave's toddler boy and girl, a Christmas bundle several years earlier. And now there was a new addition to the "Rusticii bunch"—she would be about 6 months and probably already sitting in the high chair with her big winning smile.

When life got monotonous or she couldn't stay busy enough to feel useful, and when she knew the roads were safe, she would occasionally call ahead and then joyfully climb into her beloved but aging Oldsmobile. She loved Big Red with all her heart—and loved the keys even more. How good it felt now to be on the road again after a long winter's dreariness. Summer was in the offing, and crops were beginning to grow in the sun. Such a pleasant drive.

For this homegrown, farm-raised lady, the countryside was a remembered and coveted taste of home. Now, with Royal Park condos left in the dust, she'd successfully maneuvered on over to Byron Road. Off and away—this still pretty silver-haired lady. Country air, greening fields spinning out for miles, cattle grazing peacefully in spring grasses—all of nature prepping for her favorite season: summer.

She brooded sometimes about her last years with Dad—happy years spent in their beloved motor home on Nettles Island, Jensen Beach, Florida. Mom thrived in summer heat and savored all the friends she made over the years in this southern haven. We were thankful for her younger sister, Gloria, and her husband, Curt—a retired GM engineer who kept the motor home running and up to his own high standards. We were so thankful for their close watch over these two. Dad and Curt shared a wonderful friendship and kept each other laughing and healthy, on the golf course and sharing good times with visiting friends and family.

Now Mom couldn't wait to see how those babies had grown in the last few months. *Alicia's house is just off Eighty-Fourth, and thank You, Lord!—Byron Road magically becomes Eighty-Fourth!* "A nice drive through the country," she would say.

Past neat and tidy farms and farmhouses with their acres of grass all around. Soon she recognized Byron Center's black muck fields on either side. Rigid rows of onion sets, celery, and radishes. She looked for Kapteyn's Market—just up the road. Too early for sweet corn, she told herself. Probably not open yet.

She was ecstatic to have something worthwhile to do this afternoon. She could well imagine how busy Alicia was now, with three preschoolers and one in school. Her granddaughter would be so happy to see the ironing basket emptied.

We agreed. Then we'd all send up a fervent prayer. "Gramma, Lord— she's on the move."

Once there, laundry was a key determinant—a reason for living it seemed, for new mom and me—proud Grandma Z.

Mindless ironing, hanging finished items on tiny little girl and boy hangers and Alli's darling little school-girl outfits on colored hangers, this mother of eight and grandma to forty-six was happy now to chatter away to her heart's content.

Dave's pile of rumpled dress shirts, now starched and pressed, took their place on grown-up hangers. Hands down, Dave was Gramma Great's most appreciative recipient, so thankful not to have to do his own ironing now. Mom would sympathize and promise to come again soon. He assured her she would have plenty to do.

What a blessing to feel needed! Ironing, mending—she could do it with her eyes closed. Alicia was her first grandchild, and now she mentally reclaimed the same mischievous little smiles—remembering.

"Naughty, naughty," she would say, when toys or food started to fly.

Twenty-one months after the twins were born, Alaina Mae—wispy white hair and irresistible dimples, a bit like Alli's, easily found her way into our hearts.

As a threesome, they grew together toward toddlerhood and preschool, Alaina doing her best to keep pace with Reese and Ryleigh. They were a study in groupthink. Born to set the world on fire, they were each other's willing accomplices.

All this was part of an afternoon delight for Gramma K.

As Alicia got her steps in, carrying one armload after another up and down the stairs, back and forth, I would work to get a good supper going and tackle another load of towels or the exploding mismatched "socks box."

Once divulged, "Alli's bus is coming," chaos erupted in our efforts to get everyone ready to run or hop into the stroller to make it to the bus stop. Jackets, boots, mittens, whatever it took. The bus stops, the red lights blink, the door opens, and then there are four—all screaming, hugging, kissing. What a show, free for the neighborhood five days a week!

This scene continued as long as Alaina was a preschooler—a year too long, if you asked her. Now it was three on the bus and one waiting to catch a ride with our Miss Kathy.

Alli always brought a smile to Gramma Ks face as she watched Big Sister entertain the little ones. *Was she remembering her caregiving years with the eight of us? Or long before that, her eleven younger siblings?*

All the while, Alicia and I would attempt to tune in to Grandma's continuous banter—just well enough to respond, when necessary.

Another time and a bit later, while we ran circles with laundry, after-school snack prep, and suppertime becoming an urgent consideration, three-year-old Alaina was coloring at the kitchen counter, close to where Gramma Great was ironing and talking. Alaina wondered what the spirited, one-sided conversation was all about.

Little Miss Precocious thought she should clear things up, so in her quizzical little-girl voice, she muses, "Gramma, do you know, no one is listening?" Talk continues. A little louder: "Gramma! Do you know, no one is listening?" Still no response. Frustrated, she yells, "Graamma! *Don't you know? No one is listening to you!*"

Gramma, now frustrated also, responds, "It doesn't matter, Alaina! I can talk anyway!" Alaina just shrugs her little shoulders, wrinkles her dimpled cheeks—and picks up another crayon.

Alicia and I heard it all, strangling the urge to burst out laughing.

Chalk it up as another Grandma K story. We have many. Some can be told. Others—maybe not.

Alicia always enjoyed the diversion from her daily frantic routine, and Grandma was usually welcome company. No high maintenance, this lady—as long as she was in charge of the conversation. Most times, one only had to listen, give assent, and brew another cup of tea.

Mom had abandoned her coffee addiction, years earlier. Thankfully, we were all stocked up with specialty herbal teas. Getting her to try something besides Lipton Black became a game she soon enjoyed. She loved that cute little tea basket.

***

As I write, I'm immediately taken back to my own childhood with another Grandma—my own Grandma K. We didn't need to talk much with her either. She loved it when we sat with her in the living-room. All that was required was to listen and mostly just let her know we agreed with her in spirit. Decoding this grandma's broken Dutch/English well enough to respond correctly with "uh-huh" or "uh-uh" and a proper shake of the head, was an early joyride into the world of foreign language.

Another time and place, and a very different lady. Let's brew another cup of tea, Grandma!

No such thing as herbal teas yet. Lipton reigns supreme. Or was it Salada? And don't forget: Two scoops of sugar in every cup!

Something to Ponder

> Are there stories from the past that you can smile or even laugh about now—events that bring an immediate joy response?
> What comes to mind when you think of how you might lighten the load and add a little sunshine to someone's life?

A Truly Merry Christmas!

> Some say that ever 'gainst that season comes
> Wherein our Saviour's birth is celebrated,
> The bird of dawning singeth all night long ….
> The nights are wholesome, then no planets strike, …
> So hallowed and so gracious is the time.
> —Shakespeare (first scene of *Hamlet*,
> Marcellus to Horatio and Bernardo)

Timeless lines such as these renew in us a sense of awe and wonder, too easily forgotten in our hurry-scurry, mad dash toward the event of Christmas. It's good to remind ourselves whose birthday it is and why His birthday has become the most celebrated day of the year—nearly worldwide.

In the lines above, Marcellus is speaking to his friends during a very dark and difficult season of life. He stops briefly to reflect on the holiest of historical events—when our Savior was born into a discordant world—similar to the world a young Hamlet and a wiser Marcellus knew.

We know the cruelties of our own world. Filled with terror, hatred, and revenge. We see and hear about the horrors of sin every day. Sometimes it comes close and shocks us. Sadly, some of us have experienced evil in its vile forms, as it has come directly into our homes.

For my family and for most of our community, we try to escape its ugliness by thinking of it as the world out there. We choose to live where beauty and goodness and God's grace shelter us from the brunt of the tempest and the chaos, but then it creeps into our own space, and we are fearful.

Last Christmas, our pastor's Christmas message focused on the word *merry*. As in, Merry Christmas! He reminisced about his own Canadian childhood and then his life as a warmhearted young father of three boys.

By this time, I was caught up in my own childhood memories—climbing to the top of snow piles on either side of our narrowing country road, warned repeatedly not to touch the telephone lines (probably power lines also).

Then my mind crisscrosses to when our own kids were young and seeing the miracles of Christmas—eyes wide open and innocent. Cookies for Santa, sugared treats, licking the beaters, gifts they wanted and got or didn't. Parties with cousins, grandparents, uncles, and aunts. Many are now waiting on the other side of faith.

As I write, I remember reflective times spent together, sharing songs and scripture readings and personal stories that bring to life the holiness of Christmas—as it should be or as we thought it should.

Most of Pastor Scott's audience on this Christmas Day live and breathe Pure Michigan. We hold on to memories of our snow-laced childhood or of our own children at play in the world of snow games. For our younger families, some of the best fun happens out in the snow after a Christmas feast.

Pastor Scott notes that the past several months have dumped more snow than most of us want to remember. Many of us nod, cynically. Yes, we feel dumped on … and not just with snow! We're fending off hurts that claim too much of our time—especially in this season when everyone around us seems happy and carefree. Instead, we're on our knees, praying desperately for things to be different. And with the world in such turmoil, it's hard to ignore that others are hurting as well.

When hearts are broken, the only satisfying and sustaining gift we can offer or choose to receive is God's gift of love, brought to us in the form of an innocent and immaculate Baby, born with the express purpose of setting our longing spirits forever free.

Whatever unsettles you, let it be. Let it go. Be filled with Joy. Christ has come. He is the heart of Christmas—with us now and always. Life, *your* life, is truly worth living.

Don't allow the ghosts of Christmases past to determine this or any day of your precious life. Joy to the world, and Merry, Merry Christmas!

Something to Ponder

➤ Advent, for Christ's followers, signifies the four-week period leading up to Christmas, celebrating the coming of Jesus. Where do you find your greatest satisfaction during this oft-misrepresented but holy season of Advent?

➤ It's hard to write this and not feel an overwhelming sense of guilt—and urgency. Talk with your family about what each of you can do (the little things) to dispel the darkness of those whose lives have little meaning and no hope for eternity unless someone brings the Light and tells the Story.

Green in Every Season

She is like a tree
planted by streams of water,
which yields its fruit in its season
and her leaves do not wither.
Whatever she does, she prospers.
—Psalm 1:3 (paraphrased)

Shortly after my sixty-fifth birthday I sat with a large group of women at a Beth Moore Women's Conference. I had never heard her speak live, and like the thousands of people sitting around me, I was mesmerized by the message she felt led to bring.

Beth is a well-established Bible teacher whose teaching ministry comes primarily by way of video and large women's group settings. Since that first encounter, I have sat humbly and gratefully at her feet for studies in Revelation, James, Esther, Daniel, and others.

It would be difficult to find another woman with more energy, more joyful exuberance, and equal strength of voice, presence, and character.

At this, my first encounter with Beth's in-depth teaching, she shared a unique perspective on trees. We were encouraged to contemplate and absorb lessons from *Out on a Limb*.

I knew immediately that I had found the theme for a memoir I would soon be writing.

I wrote furiously, determined not to miss a thing. I went home and, late into the night, copied page after page of scribbled notes onto my computer. I knew I would return again and again to assimilate Beth's ideas about trees into this new and unfamiliar season of my life known simply as retirement.

I gathered precious ideas for measuring my life by the standards of a good fruit-bearing tree. The message reverberates in my life every day as I make a concerted effort to live audaciously.

I discovered later that Beth had written a book titled

Audacious—about living boldly for God in a rapidly evolving and deteriorating world—a world seeking to lure us from our source of sustenance, drawing us toward mindless and frivolous activities, determined to use up our time and take away the good things God has in mind for us to enjoy.

I learned from Beth that it's not my business to work on or worry about the fruit I produce. What appears at harvest time will be as luscious and sweet as the tree is healthy and green. It is my privilege and my responsibility to care for the tree. The tree is me! I need to be firmly rooted in the well-watered soil of God's Word if I truly want to live green and healthy.

Beth reminded us that some of the fruit may not be evident until much later in life. God alone knows when the fruit is mature. My responsibility is to live a faithful and productive life in anticipation of the harvest by doing what God calls me to do each day.

I went home that night, happy to be the tree planted by the streams of living water, who will yield its fruit (gladly) in season and whose leaf will stay green for life.

From that day, everything I have written or edited is filed under the heading Living Green. It has become my audacious (as in: intrepidly daring, like a mountain climber) life theme.

Something to Ponder

> What does this essay say to you in the season of life where God has placed you or where you have chosen to grow and be productive?
> As you think about your life, where you are today, is there something that needs to change? Name it. Pray about it. Go to work!

God's Reward for Gray Hair and Wrinkles

Grandchildren are the crown of the aged.
—Proverbs 17:6 (ESV)

I have to begin this essay with some clarification. My first draft was written about seven years ago, when this year's graduates were still in grade school. Since that time, sports have become a little more—shall we say, competitive? There's more "skin in the game." And you can take that, literally. Skin and bones! But, it is fun to remember when we could simply enjoy the funny little things they did.

One of our earliest memories is of our one and only grandson (probably three or four) twirling around, picking dandelions for Mom, with his soccer teammates running down the field in hot pursuit of a toddler sized ball. He since has shown great finesse in the field of music, particularly Jazz. We travel miles to hear this boy-become-man-artist. What a joy to a Grandma with a hard-fought-and-won music major!

One way to stay young is to grow sports-focused grandkids. We have no wallflowers in this family, and a scrappy attitude is as highly valued on the team as it is opposed on the home front. This partially explains why we have so much fun at the games. On the team, scrapping is not only acceptable—it's encouraged! Go get 'em, girl!

Having seven grandkids, in four season sports, choir, band, and orchestra, means no snoozing for us. We attend every game or school concert we can fit into our fast-paced schedule.

Here's to grand parenting! We're the only team-support, besides mom and dad, huddled together in rain, sleet, snow, or the abominable humidity of a summer heat spell. If Grandpa can find a parking space with a good view of the playing field, Grandma might sit it out —inside, with heat or air, depending.

We appreciate that all these sports provide ample opportunity for great exercise routines for seniors. We can scream and yell, jump up and down like yo-yos—with few or no negative repercussions. We've also learned that parking a mile away from the gym or field is usually helpful. The more games, the better we feel! And the better we sleep!

Someone (not yet a grandparent) says, "Do you really have to go to every game and every program?"

No, we say. But, they're only young once.

Time moves on—*like an ever-rolling stream*, says the hymn writer, Isaac Watts. He reminds us how quickly the *now* becomes *too late*.

Something to Ponder

> ➤ If you have young children or grandchildren, what makes you smile as you think of them? If they are grown up, what memories linger to make you smile?
> ➤ What do they do today that makes you smile?
> ➤ How have your children and grandchildren blessed your life in who they are or have become?

Home Alone

Love can't mature in one room.
It has to come out of the full sharing of everything.
Joys, aspirations, downfalls, all of it.
That's the only real path to love.
—Leon Uris, American historical fiction writer, Trinity

When winter winds howl and snow swirls unbounded on the frozen lake, Al usually finds his way into my sacred domain, the kitchen. Usually it is TV boredom that rousts him around to the old recipe box. He loves that old plastic box with the broken hinges.

This time, his latest foray into my space takes place when, in total disgust and with loud noises, he abruptly leaves the crime scene of the Tigers' "absolute stupidity!" He has a hard time watching it all go down in flames. After a quick rundown and more loud noises, he slams the remote.

Silence! Now he's looking for a mood chaser.

It is well past Valentine's Day, and Christmas decorations high atop the refrigerator look silly. He's up for making the changes. Then he says "Let's bake a batch of cookies. I'll do the work."

"Hon—it's after nine p.m.!" Big sigh.

Oh well, why not? I'm stuck with editing this book in my adjoining office. He's got the batter mixed, and he's done it all with minimal help and only a few questions. "Is this baking soda or baking powder? What's the difference? So ... which should I use?"

"I think the recipe calls for both. Let me see ...."

All goes well—up to the last step. No rolling messy dough balls for him! But that's the fun for me—and I need a break. He's great at cleanup, so let's get those cookies in the oven so he can finish the job!

Time for the ten p.m. news and sports report.

Unbelievable! Those Tigers—"those nitwits"—somehow

turned it around and pulled off a win, and we missed it all except for the news clip!

***

A few years ago now, we were looking directly in the face of those impending retirement years. Time to get real. We had a very large house and lots of water toys——all demanding a proportionate commitment of time. We were ready to be free of the excessive responsibilities of home ownership, ready to ease into a slower-paced lifestyle——including some delightful travel experiences.

We were blessed to find the perfect condo in early rough-in stage, close by to where our kids and their families were fully established. Two years later, we moved in.

Condo living is not for everyone. Most scoff at it till their friends show off their new digs and seem perfectly content and happy—touting the freedom to roam and spend less time, energy, and money on repairs. Who needs the upkeep, yard work, monthly bills …?

For us, it works really well. We love the easy lifestyle. We still take our travel trailer out of Jerry's barn to camp all around Michigan, most times with friends and family—spring, summer, and fall. Better yet, we will soon spend our second winter in a warmer clime, golfing, visiting friends, and involving ourselves in a local church.

Come spring, we'll happily follow our hearts back home. Wherever we are, we still love our "home alone" together time. It's really not the place we settle into. It's love in the heart, shared, double.

Addendum: Now, several years down the road, I've tried to capture a picture in words of the many ways God has led us to where we are today. This year we are blessed to celebrate fifty years of marriage, twins celebrating their high school graduation with honors and a fun-filled party, and a tenth birthday celebration for the youngest among us. As life would have it, we celebrated all these events in one full-to-capacity *Party! Party!* weekend. Life is so, soooo good!

A Lamp and a Light

The human spirit is the Lamp of the Lord;
Searching every inmost part.
—Proverbs 20:27 (NRSV)

I often wake with a hymn tune or scripture verse filtering through my still inactive brainwaves. This morning, it is a song written in 1984 by present-day psalmist Amy Grant. It was the year I went back to school. I remember singing along with Amy as I drove the freeway, on my way to a music major. I was thirty-nine. Yes, it was my actual age.

As meaningful as when it was first recorded, the message of this little chorus will impact my thoughts once again today. If it is new to you, find it on her website, and she will sing it for you.

Thy Word is a lamp unto my feet and a light unto my path.
When I feel afraid,
Think I've lost my way,
Still, you're there, right beside me.
And nothing will I fear,
As long as you are near.
Please be near me to the end ....

The title and first line comes direct from Psalm 119:105 (KJV). My waking mind now begins to process what it means for God's Word to act as a lamp to my roving feet and a light for my oft-blinded eyes. It speaks volumes for those of us who have chosen to live productively, all the way to the finish line—ever *green and ever growing.*

Without the Word, there would have been no worthy seeds planted in my heart, no meaningful cultivation of my mind, and no spiritual maturing of my character.

The Word which "became flesh and lived among us" is the

undisputed Lamp and Light for God's people in this needy world. By its own authority, the Word can quell any fears you and I might have for each and every day.

Something to Ponder

> What does your mind bring to the forefront as you wake to a new day or before you fall asleep at night?
> Practice thinking about scriptural songs or verses you know or love before you say good night and as soon as you wake. It will soon become a healthy habit and will give you a lift for the day.

A Bushel and a Peck

I love you a bushel and a peck … and a hug around the neck.
A hug around the neck and a barrel and a heap …
—Frank Loesser, *Guys and Dolls*; sung by Doris Day, 1950

Mom and Dad wouldn't have seen the 1950 Broadway musical, *Guys and Dolls*. Nineteen fifty also happened to be the year I proudly went to kindergarten. I suspect they might have picked up the melody quite soon and sung or shared it with us. All these years later, I'm remembering that we sang it to our own little girls, and I'm sure they sang it to their little ones—now all but grown up or in process of becoming.

A good friend recently told me the story about the last moments she shared with her mom, a victim of Alzheimer's. Her mom had not spoken for days, and before this her muddled mind had held court over her tongue. But, just before she died, she looked directly into her daughter's eyes and said, "I love you a bushel and a peck and a hug around the neck."

God had released this aged mother's mind to share a moment of lucid awareness and a few sweet words with her daughter. What a special memory she left behind, especially when the communication had been so limited for such a long time.

Music therapists could confirm the benefits of using music for failing memories. Softly singing a few lines from a shared past, to or with an ailing parent or friend, might spark some heat to refresh a failing memory and warm a chilly day. Think what this could mean for someone whose days are often lonely, dark, and dreary!

Something to Ponder

> What sweet memories of precious times spent with loved ones have you been able to retell or relive with your family or others?

> What makes you smile when you think of someone you loved and lost?

Winter Green and Winter White

> What good is the warmth of summer without
> the cold of winter to give it sweetness?
> —John Steinbeck

Many of my friends fly south to soak up winter's sunrays in warmer climes. They callously turn their backs and try to forget what I hurry out of bed to see. This morning, my reward is a world of white, glistening with rare purity and divine blessing.

Swirling and dancing in a bridal gown of white, flurries gather on roofs and treetops, obscuring roads and untended walkways. With souls stripped to the elements, maples, birches, and oaks seem to shift under the woolly white covering, redefining themselves in crystalline splendor.

Unrelenting and unbowed, the evergreens stand firm in remarkable contrast. I love the towering trio of blue spruce outside my window—splendid and regal in summer, they now stand fully dressed in stunning winter white. In the morning sun, they position themselves like proud giant statuary.

The wind is blustery and cold, but winter-loving birds rest blissfully sheltered beneath evergreen boughs weighted down under a hoary blanket.

The lone family of cardinals appears at the busy feed station just outside my window. The male, in pulsating red, catches my attention, but soon I see the fashionably subdued, work-oriented lady cardinal. They bring joy and beauty to my day whether lackluster or sunny and bright.

Once again I succumb to the irresistible draw of a winter wonderland scene celebrated by artists, poets, and storytellers alike and immortalized in Christmas legend and lore.

The *invincible me* thinks I should bundle up and go for a brisk walk along the lakeside, but I am feeling ill-disciplined today. Thoroughly enjoying a delicious sense of warmth and tranquility,

I pour a second cup of steaming jasmine green tea and fixate once again on the winter showstopper in progress. And I have a box seat! Thank You, Lord!

"But really," someone asks, "wouldn't you cheerfully give up your wonderland window to sit poolside, sipping a frosty raspberry ice tea with your fair-weather friends?"

For now, no. But ask again in late January or early March, when the best of resolutions start to crumble. Till then, I'll soak up the joys of winter green and winter white.

Anne Bradstreet, early American English poet (1612–1672) and first colonialist to be published, would have known the hardships of winter in ways most of us can never claim, but her perspective is one I continue to embrace: "If we had no winter, the spring would not be as pleasant. If we did not sometime taste of adversity, prosperity would not be so welcome."

Perspective is everything, they say. Life is good, so very, very good!

Postscript to this essay, written in January 2013: We are five years down the road and in our early seventies. The appeal of sitting poolside sipping a mint julep or raspberry ice tea has commandeered our hearts. So at year's end we will head, once again, to Summerfield, Florida—for Al to golf and me to edit the book you hold in your hands. Till then, we will enjoy the initiation ceremony of winter, here in Pure Michigan. We'll come home, anxious to welcome the springtime overture of nature.

Something to Ponder

> What is your favorite season, and what do you love about it?
> If you are a wishful snowbird who hasn't flown south, what do you still enjoy about winter?

Where the Heart Is

> Mid pleasures and palaces though we may roam,
> Be it ever so humble, there's no place like home.
> —John H. Payne

I remember spending time at Grandma and Grandpa K's house, with cookies and tea and the old-fashioned black dominoes with tiny white-dots. Now I understand why this was so much fun for them. Their life was pretty quiet, and they appreciated the visits of grandchildren they loved. I remember hearing them laugh together. Better yet, I remember the joy of laughing with them.

Leaving home at eighteen to go to college and having little access to a car, I rarely visited with grandparents until Al and I met and we could go together. He had never had grandparents, so visiting Grandpa and Grandma, on either side of the family, was a welcome event.

Grandma K loved the word *huiselijkheid*. No one could say it with more meaning. (You have to roll the tongue on the *h* and the *jkh*.) It relates to tidying up and making everything *homey and comfy*. She didn't have much, but it was everything she needed. Still, it was always her aim to be welcoming and a good hostess. As long as she was able, she loved to show off the flower gardens in her yard and arranged fresh on her table. Of course, we never lacked for good cookies after our game—from the bakery, of course.

It's all part of the memories. Our Grandma K was all about clean and homey—*huiselijkheid*.

***

The trunk and back seat were loaded with golf clubs, a printer, computers—his and mine—foodstuffs, and mounds of luggage. Like all the snowbirds we had ridiculed in the past, we left Michigan to head for Summerfield, Florida, and a rented house with a guest room and a golf cart.

When we arrived, now three winters ago, we were amazed and humbled. We knew, immediately, our favorite space would be out on the lanai. It opened to an expansive backyard and connected to the dog run and my favorite walk path.

We laughed when we first saw our neighbors "walking their dogs" behind or alongside an ambling golf cart. Funnier yet would be the big, strong dog racing out ahead of a speeding golf cart as if he was in charge. We soon learned that the cart takes the place of an owner who no longer can, maybe never could, or now prefers not to walk his or her pet. How fast they travel depends on breed, age, and mobility of dog and owner. The cart also gives owners opportunity to socialize with other pet owners or walkers—like me. How perfect! They have their own little afternoon delight, sitting under the shade trees, dogs resting quietly—usually, just behind the pickleball court. Meet at four p.m., friends!

Brett and Sue left instructions to use anything in their well-stocked pantry and kitchen. We love cooking, so it was fun freshening up her spice rack and loading the pantry and fridge with healthy foods—for our own enjoyment, or to share with guests.

It wasn't long before we were fully acclimated to our home away from home. We've always been able to work quietly in our separate worlds, of drawings and specs or writing materials, and this open-spaced living area was a great fit. Al's computer is set up on one side of the spacious living area, and mine is on the other.

The manuscript for my first book is now in the publisher's hands, and I've been working diligently to move it to the finish line—while Al stays busy with sideline engineering or a day out on the golf course with friends.

As retired and recovering workaholics, the Zs have acquired a fondness for roaming the countryside to explore new villages, shops, beach restaurants, fruit markets, and town centers. Even

Wal-Mart and Aldi are within golf cart range, so when one of us has a yen to go somewhere, the other packs up, and we're on our way.

Evenings, if we can't find a local concert or church-sponsored event, we play Quiddler or the nameless dice game our first Florida guests taught us. We call it Dicey. When we bring out the black tablecloth with a repetitive pattern of big yellow bumblebees to cover the antique dining room table, it primes the pump for lots of good fun and laughter—best medicine ever!

Sharing time and a listening ear around the table, eating a home cooked meal, playing games or simply having a good chatfest brings out the best in all of us and serves as a mental, emotional, and psychological tune-up.

We've enjoyed traveling to many different cities, states, and countries in the past few years, and we have learned, it is possible to feel at home and where others can feel at home with you—in a hotel room, a centuries-old castle, or a humble abode with a pretty teacup sitting in a matching saucer, with a windmill cookie tucked outside the rim, with two scoops of sugar—or not!

A little effort to be hospitable can create a warm feeling of *huiselijkheid*. All you really need is a warm heart for drawing others into your life, to share meaningful conversation or fun-loving banter. Add in some hearty laughter, and you and your guests will be blessed with another joy-filled memory.

Something to Ponder

> What makes a place just plain homey? Is this important to you? Why or why not?
> When and where do you have the most fun, with the least stress and the greatest reward?
> How could you make your world just a little bit more inviting to someone who needs you to care—just a little bit more?

Not Just Another Sad Story

> He had sat at grief's table, eaten of grief's blackened
> bread and dipped his morsel in her vinegar.
> —Charles H. Spurgeon, Sermon 1099

As people called by the Man of Sorrows (Mark 8:34), we are, because of His victory over death, redeemed and transformed to share our stories of hope, healing, and renewal. With people who need answers to the reverberating *Why?*s of life—answers capable of satisfying the deep longings of grief-stricken or lonely hearts.

We are well into the season of Lent as I write. I am reminded of a *Breathe Writers* sectional I attended several years ago. It was titled, *Jesus, Man of Sorrows—Using suffering well in your fiction and nonfiction. The* facilitator was no stranger to the subject matter, as were most of us, the participants.

As an unpublished author, I soaked in as never before the importance of letting God take us to "the other side of suffering" *before* we share our most painful life storms in narrative.

As I probed through parts of a sermon entitled *Man of Sorrows*, taken from a Lenten service in 1853, the Prince of Preachers, Charles Haddon Spurgeon, reminded his audience that Jesus, our own Man of Sorrows, has proven to be more effective in relieving the world's sorrow than any other remediator in history. Troubled people turn to the cross, before they turn to Bethlehem, finding there is no tonic more effective, with greater healing power, than the redemptive story of Jesus's suffering and resurrection.

***

Stories, if you think about it, can best come alive after they have been pondered and given time for reflection. Time is the marinade that takes a story to a deeper, richer level. As in historical biographies and novels, looking back on decisions made in the course of human existence gives one a more qualified perspective. It is still and forever will be a perspective, but it can give a story a more vibrant and formational voice.

As I think about this, I am reminded that Jesus knew His disciples would have a greater physical role in sharing His message of love and redemption, because they would have the benefit of piecing together the redemption story in their own minds—after He was gone from their sight.

What we have to offer our readers is no longer just another sad story. Stories of hope and healing, because of the Life-Giver working His work in us, become formational once we ourselves are transformed.

The mystifying wonder is that the same God who wrote the Ten Commandments on tablets of stone can become the best Friend we have as we remember and possibly roll out One. More. Story.

Something to Ponder

➤ Spending time with many writers, published and not-quite-ready-to-publish, I was encouraged by the resilience and resolve that exists in each of us. We are Christian writers determined to keep the wonder alive and bring glory to His name. How is this true in your own life?

➤ Do you have a story you could share with someone? Do it! You might not ever feel ready, but He uses what you give and then turns it like the rivers of water in the direction He wishes (see Proverbs 21:1).

➤ Now that we have reckoned with the Man of Sorrows, our anticipation of his return as the King of Glory should lighten our step and brighten our day. Amen?

May the God of hope fill you
with all joy and peace in believing,
so that
by the power of the Holy Spirit
you may abound in hope.
—Romans 15:13 (ESV)

Acknowledgments

Thank you to my wonderful circle of family and friends—especially husband, daughters, sisters, and sisters of the heart. You are many. Forgive me for not validating you when you needed from me what you so freely gave to me. Thank you for being so constructive in my life.

If you are reading this page, you are a blessing to me. Many of you are fighting much larger battles than mine. I hope you enjoyed the banter and humor, as we journeyed together.

If you are a writer, thank you for sharing my walk of faith. Take anything from my pantry of words and thoughts to spice up your own writing projects––you have my blessing!

Thank you, Rasii, once again, for putting color and style to something that existed only in my mind's eye, creating a cover to draw my readers inside. I love working with you.

It is my prayer that our relationship with the One who created us for His own glory will be strengthened by having spent precious time together.

Thank God that as we fight the good fight, we become overcomers—as long as we hang on to the promises scattered all through scripture.

Mine is the walk of faith that followers of Christ commit to, but sometimes we stumble. We might even fall. But then another sojourner comes alongside and gives us a hand up.

Life pulls us in many directions, but as we are committed, so we must do—each of us, faithful to our own calling.

Count it all joy, my brothers [and sisters],
when you meet trials of various kinds,
For you know that the testing of your
faith produces steadfastness.
And let steadfastness [perseverance] have its full effect,
That you may be perfect and complete, lacking in nothing.
—James 1:2–4 (ESV)

About the Author

Anita Kraal-Zuidema was born and raised in Holland, Michigan, and earned her BA and MEd at Calvin College in Grand Rapids. She is grateful and blessed to have celebrated fifty years of marriage to Allan Zuidema this past summer. They live in Byron Center, Michigan, close by their daughters, Alicia and Amy, their husbands, and seven grandchildren. They all attend the same God-honoring church, are active participants, and are grateful to see their family grow in faith and love for the Lord in this place.

Anita's first book was titled *She Walks in Beauty and Endless Light* (2017). Her mission is, as it was then, to leave a written legacy of spiritual journeying, in short essay form, showing her love of family and friends and of God and His people. She encourages writers to take a peek inside and drink deeply to refill their own cups.

As God plants His words and thoughts into our lives, we pray that others will see His Love, shining bright and pointing *Toward Endless Light*.

You may email your thoughts to anizuid@gmail.com.

CPSIA information can be obtained
at www.ICGtesting.com
Printed in the USA
BVHW072207040719
552614BV00006B/26/P